Hunting the
SHADOW

How to Turn Fear into Massive Success

GEOFF THOMPSON

HUNTING THE SHADOW

www.geoffthompson.com

Printed and bound in Great Britain

ISBN: 978-0-95692-153-6

To Sharon, my beautiful wife, the girl of my dreams

Acknowledgements

Thank you very much to my lovely editor Lucy York who has done an amazing job in helping me to structure this book. Her notes on the first draft were succinct, precise and surprisingly insightful, and I am very grateful for her help.

Photo credits

Thank you to the Estate of Juan Muñoz for permissions and photographs of:

Last Conversation Piece, 1994–95
Bronze
Hirshhorn Museum and Sculpture Garden, Smithsonian Institution, Museum
Photograph by Lee Stalsworth
Image courtesy of the Estate of Juan Muñoz

Towards the Shadow, 1998
Resin
Private Collection
Photograph by Attilio Maranzano
Image courtesy of the Estate of Juan Muñoz

Also to my friend Mark Leverson for use of his personal photograph of *Last Conversation Piece*, 1994–95.

'Fear is the cheapest room in the house. I would like to see you all living in better conditions.'
Hafiz

Lift the self by the self
Never let the self droop down
Because the self is the self's only enemy
The self is the self's only friend.
The Bhagavad Gita

Contents

Preface

We all have shadows. All of us, even if and especially when we think we don't. Each shadow is a small bundle of death that we carry around inside us, the remnants of old wounds, of trapped emotion, burgeoning grief, simmering grudge, raging anger and ravaging guilt. Shadows are collections of exhausted life, hurts and traumas and let-downs that have been experienced but not processed and have instead formed a blockage or a sub-personality inside us. Our bodies and our minds have become like a crowded purgatory of lost souls, all looking for release. Because they are the trapped shadows of unprocessed and dead experience and they are residing in a living, flowing organism, these shadows do not serve us; in fact, they do us a disservice. The great problem is that most of us are not even aware we have shadows. And because of our ignorance we go through a life like a feral pack without a top dog.

This book is about recognising the existence of shadow, identifying our different sub-personalities and ultimately dissolving them until we are left absolute, leaving only our true self in residence.

Introduction

Let us be clear of one thing: most people think small.

The greater majority imagine small, believe small, talk and subsequently live small.

Many will violently defend their right to do so; some even kill others to protect the reality of their very small ideas.

Because of this, *most people* create small lives and settle for a quietly disappointing existence: small jobs, small relationships, small houses, small cars, small beliefs, small tolerance, small generosity and, sadly, small hearts.

This limited thinking is really not good enough! It is time to change.

Small thinking is not only old-fashioned, unhealthy and very unattractive; it is also killing us as a species. If we keep under-thinking we will go the same way of the dinosaur. That is fact.

The Universe does not think small; it is ever expanding, getting bigger with every passing second.

So… we have to stop swimming backwards, stop treading water and desist from hiding under waves of our own ignorance.

There is one reason and one reason alone for our smallness: FEAR.

Thinking, talking and living big takes massive courage.

People are afraid to think big and, because of this, all their exciting dreams of a better life sit unrealised just beyond a thin membrane of angst.

The Sufi mystic Rumi advised in his poem 'Night Traveller' that not only should we face our fears, we should actually take the initiative and go out into the night to hunt our fears down.

Hunting the Shadow is a book of empirical techniques that will enable you to recognise, face and ultimately dissolve the membrane of fear that is blocking your path to a greater life.

Chapter 1

Discomfort and Fear

In the following chapters, I will be delving into the heart (and into the art) of shadow hunting, explaining what shadow is, how to recognise it, how to draw it out into the open, how to shrink it and ultimately how to dissolve it. But before we embark on this journey, let's first talk about discomfort and fear, because when we engage in any regime of self-improvement, especially one this ambitious, we will certainly encounter this deadly duo. We will experience bodily reactions that are uncomfortable and frightening, and if we do not become their master, these feelings will defeat us at every turn. Most people who fail in any endeavour do so because they have no understanding of or tolerance for discomfort, and yet discomfort is manageable if you understand its nature. And fear – when harnessed – is the friend of exceptional people. This book, then, is about becoming exceptional, first by collecting vital information, and secondly by using that information correctly and courageously.

Climbing Everest

Like a climber on a high ascent, we will sometimes feel disoriented, we will often experience doubt and we will regularly, as a matter of course, become breathless. The air on the mountain is very thin. I would like to forearm you, at the start of your journey, with some rudimentary advice on how to deal with your own bodily reactions to confrontation; how to control anxiety and how to become a master of fear. The feelings associated with fear are unpleasant – let us be in no doubt about that – and looking for comfort in this arena will only lead to disappointment. It is better, instead, to find a change of perspective and become comfortable with discomfort by embracing the things we fear. Doing so will create a paradigm shift that will be empowering. While the right information regarding fear *will* help – because knowledge dispels fear – I have to warn you that there is no quick fix, no 'magic potion', and neither should there be. We need to respect fear and remember that it is there as a survival imperative; fear is a biological necessity, and if we want to master our bodies and our minds and sculpt an amazing life with our thoughts, then we should be prepared to find, face and embrace the things we dread most. We will not overcome monsters from our cosy beds, or from the safety of the local gymnasium. We should not seek comfort; when ascending high climbs, ease is a luxury that only the naive expect. While we do need to be respectful of fear, what we don't need to be is hypersensitive to its effects, scuttling cravenly away every time we get a drop of adrenalin.

I remember watching a wonderful documentary about a super-fit athlete who wanted to climb Everest, but like many people he wanted growth without discomfort. He trained his body in the gym to humming perfection; he was sinewy and conditioned, everything that an athlete should be. All the guy lacked was actual experience on Everest. He'd climbed a few hills to get a feel for it, but he'd never set foot on the mountain itself. His colleagues on the expedition were a group of craggy, mountain-savvy, veteran climbers, all of whom were conditioned to the harsh realities of Everest. On his first day at base camp, when his chest was as tight as a fat kid's T-shirt and he couldn't get a full breath of air, he turned to one of the stalwarts for advice. 'The air this high is thin,' he was told. 'It is always hard to breathe and a tight chest is the norm when you are on the mountain.' The next day, our neophyte, full of unrecognised adrenalin and still unable to get his lungs full, complained again. 'I'm super-fit,' he said. 'I run marathons. I do hours on the weights. I shouldn't be feeling so uncomfortable. I can't breathe properly.' Again the old lag said to him, 'Look, you're on Everest; the altitude is high so the air is very thin. None of us can get a full breath. If you wake on the mountain feeling shit, it's a good day. It's a normal day.' Still unable to take good advice and becoming ever more fearful of his bodily reactions to the mountain, the beginner said once again, 'Something is wrong with me. I must be ill. I can't breathe properly and...' The veteran, tired by now of the constant whining, cut him short and said (eyeball to eyeball), 'Listen to me. You are at altitude. *The air is thin.* If you want more air, climb a smaller mountain!'

To succeed it helps to understand that attempting high ascents (shadow hunting) will stretch you; it will be intimidating and your bodily reactions will let you know about it. This doesn't mean that you're in the wrong place. On the contrary, it means that you're in the arena. If it is not daunting, you are on the wrong path.

Ambiguity and uncertainty

It's a plus if you can eschew the need for certainty (there is rarely certainty in life) and it is a real bonus if you can look upon ambiguity and revel in it. Discomfort is the norm for the shadow hunter; he has to develop a high tolerance for uncertainty, and ambiguity will meet him at every bend until all the hills are levelled and all the valleys are filled. And here's the thing about developing a high tolerance for ambiguity and uncertainty: it makes you grow. That's what it does. The discomfort of facing your fears, of being active in the gap between desire and inertia, is like fertiliser for the soul; when you sit in it you expand. This is the secret; this is where the alchemy lies and this is why managing fear is the very first lesson in shadow hunting.

Almost everyone avoids discomfort; most actively run away from and resist it and because of this they fail to grow. Organisms will only evolve if they actively seek out evolution or if they (as the mystic and spiritual teacher G. I. Gurdjieff said) pursue *conscious labour and deliberate suffering.* In order to evolve, we have to be active. Like a bodybuilder who wants to build muscle, we must consciously and deliberately place ourselves into situations again and again that demand growth. A bodybuilder will employ resistance exercises (using weights) to break down muscle tissue in order to force the muscle to re-knit more strongly. Similarly, if we want to grow intellectually, morally, ethically or spiritually we too have to place ourselves into situations that demand growth. It is the very act of indecision (that deliciously uncomfortable place between *Shall I?* and *Shall I not? Can I?* or *Can't I? Will I?* or *Won't I?*) followed by action, and the discomfort this creates, that develops not just us but a separate part of us. A physically weak man who uses the power of his will to place himself in a weightlifting gym develops a separate, strong self. It is because of discomfort and not despite it that he is able to do this. As our *separate self* grows and becomes stronger, we are able to take on bigger and more demanding challenges. This is the same in any arena. A frightened man with a desire to find courage but neutralised by fearful inertia will develop a separate warrior self simply by stepping onto the battlefield and successfully facing his enemy. Before the battle there is a scared man; after the battle there emerges a new man, the warrior.

Looking for the burn

The place that everyone avoids, the uncomfortable space between desire and inertia (see Chapter 2, The Power Triune), is the actual forge where all growth occurs. A seasoned bodybuilder knows that the 'burn' (the painful sensation experienced at the point where the muscle breaks down) is necessary for the growth of the muscle to take place, so he gets into the burn as quickly as he can and stays there for as long as possible. He will even use specific techniques and exercises designed to keep him at that point of burn for longer. This ensures that he achieves maximum growth in the shortest period of time and with the least possible effort. Where many less experienced people might spend longer in the gym, consciously or unconsciously avoiding the burn (and subsequently never growing much of a physique), the stalwart will perhaps spend only forty-five minutes training, the majority of that time in the burn. When I was training for my judo black belt I devised a system of training with weights that brought me incredible stamina in a very intense session lasting only fifteen minutes; I got into the burn immediately and I stayed in it for the full duration of my training routine.

Because the bodybuilder associates the burn with growth, his perception of that agony changes and he learns to look for and love the pain. If we can change our perception of the emotional and spiritual burn that comes with managing fear, associating it instead with growth of character, we too can learn to become comfortable with discomfort, even growing to love it instead of recoiling and complaining that we are being needlessly tortured by an unjust life, an unfair society or a God of wrath.

The only caveat I would add here is this: don't do too much too soon. Growth needs to be organic and not rushed or forced. If you walk into a gym and try to lift too much weight too quickly you may be injured. All growth is the same. Don't rush it. Build your will gradually, step by steady step, layer by careful layer. And make sure, like a weightlifter, that you nourish your growth with a steady diet of inspiration (books, tapes and conversations) and rest (most new muscle growth takes place during rest and sleep). If you're going to embrace the path of conscious labour and deliberate suffering, make sure you are meticulous with your inspirational and dietary input, and that you have lots of respite, so that the muscles (physical, mental, spiritual) can recuperate and grow.

Killing your addictions

This process takes a lot of energy, and energy is one thing that a lot of people seem to be lacking. They seem to generate just enough to (just about) sustain themselves – some people don't even produce enough for that – and subsequently they become weak and ill. This is due to the fact that most people are continually having to produce enough energy to feed their uncountable addictions (food, drink, people-pleasing, pornography – all forms of shadow,

as we will see later in Chapter 3, Understan
and many more have their power devoured by un.
and uncontrolled fear (fear, or adrenalin, uses up c
amounts of energy needlessly if it is not controlled), so al
their power is spread across and lost in many divergent habits
and fears. A person who can only just sustain themselves has
no energy left for the creation of dreams. Gurdjieff believed
that every person should be able to create energy enough to
produce income and sustenance for a hundred people. He
or she should be like a small industry, creating copiously.
As I said, the majority can only just create enough to keep
themselves, and many struggle with that. How much do you
create? This is worth thinking about; it is very inspiring to
imagine that with the right conditions you can create ninety-
nine times more than you are creating right now. And just
the act of thinking ninety-nine times bigger will automatically
place your creativity in a different space. When you think
about creating enough just to sustain yourself, you will likely
as not create just enough; there is no necessity to think any
bigger than your need. But if you think about creating for two
people, or three or a hundred or ten thousand, then of course
your thinking is going to expand proportionately. When I was
in my old house, a very lovely but small abode, the mortgage
was tiny and in our business catalogue we only had eleven
products. All I had to do was create enough to make that
monthly mortgage payment, so eleven products was just fine;
it was just enough. When I moved to my next house, a lovely
big detached place, I had to find three times as much monthly
income and my output expanded massively; I created another
nineteen products, books and martial arts DVDs, taking us to
a catalogue of thirty products in all inside the next three years.
By expanding the need, I expanded my production.

The good news is, as you sack your addictions and manage your fears you will gain (or save) more and more energy, until in the end your energy will be boundless. You will have so much energy you will be able to build empires.

Understanding fear

I'd like to make one thing very clear: we do not wrestle with our fears, and we do not go to war with our addictions or our shadows (I'll go into detail about exactly what shadows are in Chapter 3, Understanding Shadow). This is not about fighting, and is not a battle or an internal conflict (even if it feels like it sometime is), certainly not in the usual sense. In the Bible it says 'resist not evil' (Matthew 5:39). In other words, don't resist your fears and addictions – don't stand at the gate and try to batter them back. Instead, give yourself to them, own them, sit them down, embrace them, make them a cup of tea, lean into those very sharp edges and you will see that what you embrace will dissolve. Conversely, what you resist will persist.

Fear is a constant in life, we all know that much, especially for those of us who wish to find sovereignty over the self, so it helps to know the workings of the adrenals, how to deal with them when they trickle and when they gush. We need to know how to slow the adrenals when they rampage, how to release adrenalin from the system when we're flooded, and how to act as a strong conduit for adrenalin and use it as a creative force.

If we fail to arrest and utilise adrenalin, the worms of decay will start working on us from the inside out.

Physiologically this is how fear works: when a confrontation of any kind occurs in our life the body transfers from homeostasis (our normal, healthy balanced state), what is known as the Parasympathetic Nervous System (PNS), into 'fight or flight', or – in physiological terms – the Sympathetic Nervous System (SNS). As soon as we find ourselves here the body floods with a cocktail of stress hormones that prepare us for a survival situation, the classic fight or flight. And in fight or flight our immediate survival instinct is to run for our lives, freeze or, if cornered, fight. If the situation is a physical threat then flight would absolutely be appropriate, and if cornered then fight might be necessary too. But as we all know, very few stressful situations in contemporary society demand that we fight, flee or freeze. If booked to do a talk on stage, running away would not be appropriate, and you can't physically fight stage fright. A deadline at work will trigger the release of adrenalin, but there is no behavioural release for it because there is no actual physical threat. There is no cheetah ballooning in front of us, teeth bared and salivating. As far as our blind, antiquated adrenal glands are concerned, however, there could be! If they are fired into action it is for one reason and one reason alone: there is a real threat to the organism and an immediate and violent response is not only necessary, it is vital!

The General Adaptation Syndrome (GAS)

Currently the human race is in a mess because we have become a *sympathetic sensitive* species (our Sympathetic Nervous System has become hypersensitive to perceived threat). And let us be very clear about one thing: the stress response is not kind to the body. Adrenalin is poisoning us; the chemicals released in fight or flight, especially cortisol, act as a caustic to the smooth internal muscles (heart, lungs, intestines, bladder, etc.). It even travels to the brain, where it attacks neurotransmitters, killing millions of cells. This is especially so if we experience lots of stress without any behavioural release, or in other words if we get stressed but there is no physical action to release the stress from our system. Imagine if you're feeling stressed several times a day, but you are doing nothing physical to release that stress. Where do you think it goes? While your system will eventually return to homeostasis (normal balance), it will still be loaded with adrenalin. In psychology this is called the General Adaptation Syndrome (GAS). When you experience stress the body goes into Sympathetic Nervous System, and when it senses that the external stressor has gone it tries to rebalance itself as quickly as possible, and goes back to the normal Parasympathetic Nervous System (balance). The chemical cocktail that was released into the body but not behaviourally used is still there, looking for an explosive physical outlet! Eventually, over time it will work its way out of your system in the normal process of everyday living; in the meantime your body is full of caustics that you either internalise, causing possible ill health, or displace inappropriately in road rage, arguments, tantrums, etc. Because the body is already adrenalin-loaded, it also becomes more susceptible to future stress, and even the most innocuous situation could become the trigger for a disproportionate adrenal release. The results of this are evident; we see them in the newspapers and on the news every day: people being attacked, even killed by highly stressed individuals, often for something as simple as jumping the queue in a shop. In the news recently was the story of a hyper-stressed lady attacking a stranger at a supermarket checkout because she was unpacking her shopping too slowly. More familiar is the husband or wife who collects stress all day at work, and then explodes in anger at home when their partner or child spills a drink, or talks while the TV is on. This of course can get you into a lot of trouble; you might lose your health, your job, your wife, your liberty – even your life can be threatened or lost if you spill your angst in the wrong direction. I know many people with failed health, failed marriages and failed lives because of adrenalin that has not been properly managed.

Managing stress is easy enough in principle, but very hard to put into practice because it takes a strong will, and a strong will needs to be developed.

Here are a few simple tips for managing adrenalin, bearing in mind that this subject is a book in itself. For more detail, refer to my books *Stress Buster* and *Fear: The Friend of Exceptional People*.

Breathing

People who are stressed tend to take shallow breaths or even unconsciously hold their breath. The brain associates this with (or mistakes it for) an external threat and triggers fight or flight, taking us into the Sympathetic Nervous System. In times of stress, breathe slowly, take a good four seconds to fill your lungs, hold the breath for four seconds, then release again, taking four seconds to exhale (this is called diaphragmatic breathing). And generally, in your everyday life, take fewer breaths per minute and you will keep stress at bay. If you are feeling stressed check out your breathing and you'll find that you are probably taking shallow breaths. Sometimes when I am at the computer I find myself unconsciously holding my breath as I type. When you recognise this, take over the breathing process manually and take long slow breaths.

Slow down

Speed triggers the adrenals. It's a fact. It tricks them into thinking that there is an external threat so they go to work.

When you slow everything down the adrenals think, Ah, everything is cool again, the threat has gone, let's relax. So... slow down. Slow everything down. Slow your thoughts down, slow your talking down, slow your walking down and slow your day down. Slow everything down. It makes economical sense because you always get more done when you are controlled and measured, and you don't wreck your health in the process. This is a very Zen-like practice. Taking control of everything and slowing it down can even turn painting a fence into a pleasurable art.

When we hurry, when we rush, when we leave late for appointments and when we fail to manage our day and leave ourselves with too much to do in too little time we are courting disaster. We are definitely courting stress, and this is the kind of drama that shadows feed on.

If the adrenals are already firing on all cylinders and you want to manually switch them off, you can do so by deliberately slowing down your breathing and your movements.

It is good habit to book-end your day with something very slow, like archery, meditation, yoga, t'ai chi or a slow walk (hand in hand with your partner is a very beautiful pastime, or walking with your dog – not hand in hand of course, that would be wrong) around a country park, or even having a quiet cup of tea in your back garden.

If you begin your day fast, with a strong coffee, a sugary cereal and the morning news (all of which will trigger the adrenals) you have already got off to a bad start, and the chances are the rest of the day will follow in a similar order. By the time you get back home at night you will be one big ball of nervous energy. This will probably leave you snapping at your partner, shouting at the kids and kicking the dog. Then you'll sleep badly because you are still filled with stress (which will make you feel as though you're on a starting block ready to run a race) and also because of the guilt associated with your bad behaviour. And you will no doubt wake up feeling shit because your partner (if you have one) has given you the cold shoulder in bed and your dog has taken himself out for a walk (because he doesn't want to get kicked again) and of course your kids (for those of you with kids) learn very quickly to avoid you when you are snappy, which layers sadness on top of your stress.

Meditation

My day starts and ends with meditation. I sit down, I listen to my breathing and I empty my mind. I do this for about half an hour each session. It's a discipline and it is not an easy one to get into, but once you start the results are little short of miraculous. Meditation has many benefits: it develops spirituality, it expands your conscious net so that you can catch bigger and better ideas and intuitions, it develops the spirit (what is known as the Atman, the God that resides in our chest) which makes us want to aspire to be thoroughly decent people, it connects us with our Source (God, the Flow, the Universe) and on the very basic level meditation triggers the Parasympathetic Nervous System, homeostasis, our natural balance. And for this reason alone meditation is well worth the effort.

If you start you day slowly with meditation (or the likes) then the rest of the day is likely to follow suit. It has certainly proven true for me.

How to meditate

There are many methods of meditation, and I encourage you to check them out to find one that suits you. My own method is simple; I sit in the middle of a quiet, dark room, on a cushion. I make sure that I feel comfortable. I switch off all the phones and ask my family not to disturb me for any reason, for at least thirty minutes. This is important; if you feel as though you might be disturbed you will not find a deep meditation. I breathe deeply and slowly for about ten breaths; this activates the Parasympathetic Nervous System which slows everything down. Once I am settled I concentrate on my breathing. I follow the breath as it comes slowly in, and I follow it as it slowly goes out. If thoughts try to invade my concentration, I simply observe the thoughts and say to myself 'thinking', and then go back to concentrating on following my breath in and out. It takes a lot of concentration, and the urge to follow thoughts and stories and imaginings is often strong, but I resist it and keep my mind focused completely on the in and out of my breath.

After a few moments the thoughts tend to desist and I am left with nothing but stillness and silence. This is the ideal place to stay for the duration of a meditation. It has a tremendous healing effect on the body and mind, it allows negativity (shadows) to be released and it actually nurtures your centre, the part that is the real you.

There are lots of books on meditation in bookshops, online and in the library. I'd recommend Deepak Chopra, the author of a number of excellent books and tapes on all things spiritual.

A word of warning: don't over-meditate. Too much trance and not enough dance is not good for you, not least because it won't leave you any time to live.

What you eat

Food is a sensitive issue. It is one of the most important things in our life and yet, the moment the importance of food in health is mentioned, people get upset and offended. My advice is this: if diet is a sensitive issue for you, get your head out of your hind. If you want health and you want happiness and you expect longevity and a degree of peace during your brief sojourn on this spinning planet, get your food right. If you put shit in, you will feel shit and you will get shit back out again. You will become a perpetuator of shit. That, my friends, is not the correct way to live, unless you like living in shit, in which case skip this section and try and find one (preferably in a softer book, one that tells you what you want to hear and not what you need to hear) that suits you better. What you eat, how you eat, where you eat and how much you eat affects the adrenals. If you eat the wrong foods, or even too much of the right foods, it places a lot of stress on the digestion and lots of energy is wasted (energy that is needed in order to be ninety-nine times more productive!) in digesting food that does nothing but store in and on the body as fat. It triggers the adrenals; it disempowers you. In the Kabala it says that all of our power is locked into our addictions. Food is a pandemic addiction; overeating kills millions each year, and for those that it doesn't kill it can be the cause of ill health. What you place in your stomach does not just affect who you are, it actually *is* who you are. The moment you ingest it, you are it. You are the double cheeseburger, you are the beer, you are the fried breakfast, and you are the drugs. In hunting the shadow this is an important lesson because, guess what: when you overindulge, it is not you that you're feeding. It's your shadow, that negative sub-personality (a separate, often

31

secret or hidden and sometimes uncontrollable part of you that is not congruent with who you really are or who you would really like to be) that wants instant gratification, the part of you that doesn't care about long-term health, only short-term highs. This is the idiotic and abusive shadow that can read 'SMOKING KILLS' in bold red type, emblazoned across the front of a cigarette packet, and still take out a cigarette and smoke it, somehow believing that the warning does not apply to them. This is a shadow that will drag you into anger and jealousy and excess; it will lure you into affairs; it will entice you into drugs; it will seduce you into dishonesty and kid you that there will be no consequence to your actions.

If your aim is self-sovereignty, then you need to shoot through several layers of consciousness to get this point across.

The key is simple with diet. Eat light. You already know the foods that are good for you and the foods that are bad. You don't need some cherry-faced doctor who likes a tipple in the afternoon to tell you that that drinking red wine is healthy, and that a little bit of what you fancy does you good. You are the person you need to listen to, or rather, your intuition and your experience. What are your reference points? How has history informed you? We are all individuals, of course, and what some of us find poisonous, others find perfectly palatable. I can't drink alcohol, not even in moderation. Alcohol is a poison for me, so I abstain completely. I can eat a moderate amount of dark cocoa chocolate and it feels fine. A friend of mine, on the other hand, likes a glass of wine, but she can take it or leave it; her life is not controlled by it and sometimes she won't have a drink for months. She can't eat chocolate though, not even in moderation, because it simply doesn't suit her. Two squares of chocolate are too much and lead to massive cravings, and three bars are not enough, because once her cravings start her appetite becomes voracious. You need to become Guinea Pig A in your own life; experiment with yourself and find out what works for you and what doesn't, discover what makes you feel alive and light and what drags your mood down and makes you depressed. If you are brutally honest with yourself and you do a food inventory you will lose most of your negative eating habits in a heartbeat.

An exercise in abstinence

Why not try this as an experiment: go without alcohol for the next three months (or your favourite food if you don't drink). See how your body resists and fights you when you first start, watch the effect it has on your friends and family, and note how they react. See if they embrace your abstinence or if they attack it. Note also how much better you feel in yourself, how much mental strength you gain from abstaining and how individual you feel, resisting a known poison in the case of alcohol (a killer of millions of men and women) that practically the whole of society is addicted to.

Start now. If you are really serious about losing your shadows, start by making your body inhospitable for them: starve them out. If you stop feeding the black dog he will soon move off to a more obliging host.

Where and how you eat is also very important. You've heard it a million times, I am sure, but eating on the go, eating fast, eating in front of the TV and eating and talking at the same time causes all sorts of digestive problems, and this is a major cause of stress and illness in society. Make eating a solitary affair, respect your food and respect your body and don't try and fit your meals into an already bulging schedule.

Your influences/impressions

People tend to think of diet as simply involving the food we eat. In actual fact everything we think, imagine, sense, see, hear, smell and touch are a part of our diet because everything we ingest becomes chemical the moment it enters our systems. It becomes a part of us, flesh, bone and sinew. This should be obvious to us all. Everything that is taken into the body and accepted becomes you. The tabloid porn you read in your daily newspaper becomes you, the 'bad news' that you watch morning, noon and night on the TV becomes you, the conversations you have over the dinner table at work or in the pub become you, as do the billboards and the posters and the films and TV that you spend probably a third of your waking life swallowing and digesting. Your reality literally consists of everything you take in on a daily basis, and your shadows live or die on all of it. It is no wonder so many of us are anxious all the time, when almost everything we ingest feeds anxiety! This is the one area that, if controlled, really can make a huge difference. The physical food we digest and the air we breathe can be cleaned up and refined, and this will have a major effect; but more than that, changing your impressions, your influences, for those of the highest calibre can be transformational. This is something that you can effect immediately. In fact, reading this book is the start of that change, because it will leave you feeling informed and empowered. This alone will starve out and dissolve shadows. So make your body and your mind inhospitable for negativity. Blow it out of your orbit by taking yourself (via your daily habits) to a high altitude.

Did you know that there is a certain variety of goose that only breeds at altitude, and it only breeds at altitude because it knows that its predators, the animals in the wild that prey on its young, can't survive in those conditions? I love this because it is how we need to live if we are to stop our shadows from growing and from inhabiting us; we have to take ourselves to a high mental altitude so that they can't get anywhere near us.

Have you ever noticed how seductive negative company can be and yet how shit and disempowered you feel afterwards? It can be hugely destructive, and sometimes it creeps up on you so quickly that you hardly notice it happening.

I have a very close friend who fell in love with and married a good-looking man who had a desperately low self-esteem. It almost ruined her whole life. While her new husband gave the false impression of being confident and outgoing, deep down he was a terrified, jealous and vitriolic little boy. This made for a violent cocktail. He became threatened by the fact that she was very close to his family, so he accused her sister of coming on to him (she didn't, she was just tactile) so my friend became quiet and withdrawn around his family. He then extended his accusations, one by one and over a period of time, to most of her friends, accusing them of coming on to him behind his wife's back. She believed him; why wouldn't she, he was her husband. So she took his side and ended up either blatantly falling out with her friends or just withdrawing from them, not answering their calls and crossing them off her Christmas card list. And her husband insisted on having naked massages by a female masseuse at their home while she was at work, and expected her not to be upset by it. Trying to be the modern woman, she suppressed the anxiety this caused her until, eventually and inevitably, it erupted in arguments and fights. One negative influence and my friend became a complete and utter stranger to me, to her family and to pretty much all of her friends. In defending her lying husband she fell out with all of her best influences, who quietly tried to tell her the truth. Inevitably they ended up in the divorce courts, but not before she lost a few very important things (friends, respect, dignity, etc.) that she has had to work very hard to get back.

On a more positive note, have you ever noticed how, when you find yourself in positive company, you come away feeling as though you could change the world? You bump into an old friend and he gives you a book to read – it has changed his life, he says – called *The Elephant and the Twig* (by a splendid writer called Geoff Thompson). You read it and digest it and suddenly you realise that, actually, *I really can change the world if I want to.* You have ingested a book and that book has become a part of you. It is chemicals in your body and brain. It is inspirational fuel. It is a mind-expanding healthy stimulant that is as much a part of you as your right arm.

My wife had this effect on me. I met Sharon when I was working in a violent job (bouncer) and living a very fruitless existence. Her influence transformed me into the man that I always knew I could be.

All this is because *you are the company you keep.* You are (literally) your influences. What you ingest you become. Everything that you take in you adopt, and if you take it in habitually it will become an established part of your milieu; in fact, if you are meticulous with your habit, it will become your whole reality.

Becoming a bull

There's a lovely old Zen tale about a monk who can't find enlightenment, and the fact that he can't find it becomes an obsession; it's all he can think about. He goes to see his master and he tells him his story. The master tells him to go to his cell, lock himself in, and spend the next week thinking about one thing and one thing only; becoming a bull. 'Think about becoming a bull, meditate on becoming a bull, talk to yourself about becoming a bull and imagine yourself becoming a bull. Spend every waking hour in this contemplation.' The monk does as he is instructed and a week later the master visits him in the cell. 'Come out here,' says the master, 'and tell me what you've learned.' The monk shakes his head, dismayed, 'I can't come out there master,' he says. 'I've tried already; I can't get my horns through the door.'

The monk finds instant enlightenment.

What you think about obsessively and emotively, what you input all day long, you will become. And your impressions, your influences, are a major part of what you input. Do you want to become a bull and get stuck in a small room because of the size of your (imaginary) horns? If you don't, then stop thinking about becoming a bull, and stop letting other people tell you that you are a bull. If you are tired of only earning a pittance, stop telling yourself (and stop letting others tell you) that you are only worth a pittance. If you want to be healthy, stop telling yourself how unhealthy you are. If you desire success, stop telling yourself that you are a failure, and never allow others to keep you in an unsuccessful place with their negativity. And if you don't want to be fearful... stop telling yourself how scared you are!

Contemporary psychologist Mihali Chicksentmihalyi (author of *The Flow*) said that our brains are bombarded by about four million bits of information, but we are only able to process 200 of them at any one time, and that 200 bits of information is what constitutes our truth. And while the reality we experience every day is true (negativity in the news, all over our newspapers and TV screens), it is only partially true. If the 200 bits of information we process are all accessed from the news, the newspapers and the word of our (well-meaning but negative) friends and family, and they are all talking pessimism, then of course our reality – our very small 200-bit reality – is going to be of a pessimistic nature. If, however – like me – you choose *not* to watch the news morning, noon and night and instead look further afield for your sustenance, your 200-bit reality can be bespoke and empowering.

Reality is being created and recreated, underlined and underscored, hashed and rehashed with every new bit of data we receive and process.

Change the information that you digest as a daily staple and you will change your world. Stop accepting and processing the same statistics as everyone else and start searching for the information (that is out there, that has always been out there and that will always be out there) that offers a more abundant road map.

The information we are continually being offered in the world's media is creating a lot of fear in people. And fear (of course) triggers the fight, flight or freeze syndrome, which in turn feeds our shadow. Rather than look objectively at the news, we try to fight it, we run away from it or we simply freeze in terror and accept the inevitable.

But we don't have to. No one is making us accept the begging bowl of famine, no one is forcing us to live fearful lives; we can go out there and discover our own feast.

There has never in the history of the world been a better time to invest in you. And a big part of that investment is choosing powerful influences.

Just because the majority want to paddle and peddle in misery, just because they choose to accept the dietary staple offered abundantly by the media, and just because they decide to believe that the 200 bits of information (out of possibly billions) *is reality* (like believing that one line from one book, in a million libraries, is the gospel) does not make it true, but if you ingest it without opposition it will probably become true for you. Listen to the prophets, the saints, the mystics and the scientists; we create and we recreate reality every day: our reality. Our reality, however, is but one room in a house of a million rooms, and by training ourselves to access new information we can ease ourselves into them all. We can even get out of the house.

Start here (this is information), raid the libraries, surf the rapids of the information highway, be a busy bee in the bookshops. Change your 200 bits of information daily by reading and watching and marinating in new data – there are people out there waiting to give it to you (many for free!). Everything is information!

Back to the basics: What you ingest via your physical food and your influences and impressions can trigger fear and feed shadow. So let's start the starvation process, and also let's start feeding our positive self, our top dog, with the best that the world has to offer.

Physical training

No matter how balanced a life you live you will have stress hormones in your body. There are more neurological stressors in society today than ever before. The majority of the things that scare us most are not real; they are little more than perceived threats, not the real-life assaults that ancient man might have experienced in the wild. Today, with all our labour-saving devices and our made-for-comfort lives, it is hardly necessary to move physically at all any more, other than walking from the house to the car and then from the car to the workplace or from the workplace (across the corridor) to the canteen, so stress hormones and bodily residues struggle to find a healthy behavioural release. Because of this our veins and arteries clog up like log-jammed motorway systems and our Formula One bodies hardly ever get off the hard shoulder. It is believed that prehistoric man covered at least eight miles every day hunting and foraging for food, and in the process not only made room for his moderate calorific intake but also burned up all and any unhealthy residues held in his body. Technologically we have developed massively since man roamed the plains with arrow and spear, but physiologically we have hardly advanced at all. Our bodies still work in pretty much the same way now as they did back then; our primitive adrenals are still on high alert looking for the sabre-toothed tiger, and they still release adrenalin if a threat is perceived, but because we no longer hunt and forage and cover our eight daily miles, the body has no natural outlet for all the stress hormones and bodily residues that build up over a day. And this is the basis for most of our physical and mental ills. We need a behavioural outlet for stress or it will kill us.

Physical training on a daily basis offers your body a surrogate release for stress; it helps the residues to find their way out of the body in the form of spent fuel. The process is a very simple one, but it does require a lot of discipline to bring a physical workout into your life and keep it there consistently. But, and this is the beauty of long-term physical training, once it becomes habit and you feel and see the benefits it gets easier and easier. In the end you will find it easier to train than not, the pain will be replaced by pleasure and your sessions will become one of the best parts of living in a human body.

I don't think it really matters what type of training you do, as long as it doesn't become too stressful or too competitive; if it does then it might create more stress than it releases. What works for me is running. It is meditative (for people with depression it has proven to be more effective than taking anti-depressants), it is empowering (it releases lots of endorphins, the natural feel-good drug in the body, and you always get a feeling of achievement when you finish) and it makes you sweat, so it releases all the trapped stress hormones from your body. And it is a very good weight regulator – running really burns the calories. But pretty much any healthy activity that gets you sweating is a very good release for stress. Again, it needs to be consistent.

Hard physical training is one of the things that make your body inhospitable for shadow. And, of course, it grows the will.

Service

It may sound corny or even contrived, but a great way to avoid and relieve stress, to lessen fear and to melt discomfort, is to serve others. I find that when my purpose is honourable, and I think about serving others more than myself, fear and discomfort lessens, and sometimes it disappears all together. Altruistic purpose is massively empowering. Philanthropic acts, particularly the kind that are neither announced nor publicly rewarded, are the very best form of service. If you do it out of a sense of duty, you bring expectation to the table and if that expectation is not met, it creates stress. If you do it for praise, it will also create stress, because sometimes you will get praise, and other times you won't, and this might leave you feeling as though you are being taken for granted. This equals more stress. And let's be honest here: public praise for being charitable is egoistical, it just feeds shadow. Do it for love; do it because it feels good to help; do it because it is the right thing to do. You'll probably get praised anyway, but don't make that your purpose. When you do, the rewards will be a hundred times greater. By serving others from love, you actually feel love. In fact, you become love. This is not about the word itself; it is about the state of being, about the frequency we tune into when we access love, which I will delve into in more detail in later chapters.

What is it that you are looking to do now? Right this minute. What goal would you really love to achieve but can't envision? I'll guarantee that between you and your dream lies one thing: fear. It is not only obscuring your view by blocking the light, but it is also scaring you out of the idea with large injections of adrenalin. Your shadow is sitting somewhere inside you, gorging on a regular diet of comfort and junk food and negative stories, waiting and watching for you to try and change the norm. And the moment you make an attempt to do so, the shadow does what the shadow always does: it frightens you with horror stories and sends you scuttling back into the centre of your comfortable (but unhappy) place. And you scurry back for one reason and one reason alone: you are afraid of the feeling of fear. You are not afraid of succeeding or failing or looking a fool or having too much responsibility. I would even say that you are not really afraid of death. You are simply afraid of your own bodily reactions. You are fearful of fear. And your shadow knows this, and so uses fear as its main arsenal to keep you where you are. But let me tell you this: the moment you start walking towards your fear instead of away from it, the moment you fully intend to break out of your fearful place, the moment you lock on to full purpose, that feeling will disappear like the morning mist. I guarantee it. Fear is perpetuated by the fear of fear. It is a vicious cycle that will stop whenever you decide it needs to stop. And when you start clearing shadows, the cosmos will open up to you. It will be like someone has turned on the lights and allowed you to see your inheritance for the very first time.

Facing fear, being a warrior and courting altruism are worthy endeavours, we all agree on that I am sure, but they are not the undertakings of the many, they are the quest of the few. It is a very courageous person who takes himself on in a fight for sovereignty, because facing your own fears is harder than facing a starving mob at a free barbecue. So, if you decide to embark on this path (and I hope that you do), then you will need all the power you can muster, especially the power of will. The best way to develop will is to place yourself in the crucible between desire and inertia. Let's look at that now.

Chapter 2

The Power Triune

Before we take a look at understanding, hunting and dissolving shadow, I'd like to share a few words with you on the development of willpower, because nothing works without will. If you don't have a strong will, don't worry, because it can be developed; it can be grown and like iron ore it can be tempered in the furnace of action.

We have all (I am sure) experienced a desire to succeed at something, and we may even have taken the first vital step towards our goal but then found ourselves without the power to begin, carry on or complete what we started. No sooner do we feel the desire to change, when a great wave of inertia sweeps over us and our desire is washed away and dissolved. We get excited about an idea, we decide to change our world, but a few days later motivation has gone. We are left feeling weak and impotent. The more times this happens, the more powerless we feel, because we get a history of defeats behind us. Failure becomes a habit; it becomes our norm. This usually occurs because we've not developed a will strong enough to move us from desire to action. And, as Einstein famously said, nothing happens in the universe until something moves. In this case that something is you. When you move, the cosmos responds. And when you move vigorously, it responds with vigour. People who lack the willpower to act often go out into the world to try to find willpower, in a book perhaps, or in a motivational talk, or maybe they seek out some mysterious guru or swami who offers them (at a price) a secret code or mantra or prayer that might unlock their vast reservoirs of power. Others still sit in meditation for hours and chant 'Om' lots of times, searching for the same elixir. It rarely works. The truth is not (as they say) 'out there'; the truth is a lot closer than you might imagine.

In my early days, when writing books and films was a distant dream, and my shadow took the form of massive self-doubt, I tried everything to overcome my uncertainty, other than the one thing that would actually make the difference. Whenever I put pen to paper the voice of my doubting Thomas rose up and reminded me (over and again) that I was wasting my time, that I was a fool to think I could be a writer, that actually I was being very pretentious. When the *negative me* rose up and confronted my emaciated will, my fledgling desire was quickly swallowed up and I put the pen down and wallowed in yet another defeat. This voice was so strong that it added bite to the bark of that dog inertia, and my will cowered. Usually, only a few lines into the writing, the shadow would take residence and I'd find myself ripping my work up and thinking, What's the point? Later, as my confidence grew, I was able to quieten that voice by developing the will to *make* myself sit down and *make* myself write, no matter how loudly it screamed its vitriol.

I learned through experience and practice that this sub-personality relied on my attention for its sustenance, and if I gave it enough attention it would take me over completely and leave me feeling depressed or angry. However, without my attention it would shrink and die. And of course, later still when success came calling and I won a few awards, my confidence expanded and left no room in my mind for such depreciation. Success culled my internal nay-sayer. When it said, 'You can't write; who do you think you are?' I'd say, 'Actually, I am a BAFTA award-winning writer so you can fuck off!' And invariably it did. Before that, in the days when success was still just in my mind's eye, this was not so easy, so solid willpower had to be developed. Reading motivational and inspirational biographies of great men and women who won through against difficult – sometimes impossible – odds helped (more on this in a later chapter); they were my main source of fuel. They filled me with the energy needed to get through another day. But ultimately it was the exercising of my will that actually developed my will. Will is forged through action; it is not formed on the settee or from the pillow in your bed.

Desire and inertia

The power of will does not actually exist at its full potential until wilful acts are undertaken. Will is developed when you place yourself between the opposing forces of desire and inertia and you act. It is in uniting this triune that real power is created.

Each of these three forces on its own is powerless. Will is impotent if you don't have anything to be wilful about.

Desire can't create without the will to act. And inertia doesn't even come into play until you try to create something. When you feel desire to lift weights and grow a physique, inertia will usually try and dissolve your desire the moment you go near a gym. If you place your will in the gap between desire and inertia (in other words, if you force yourself to lift weights and train, even though inertia is desperately trying to put you off and everything inside you is saying, 'Don't lift weights!'), you'll develop a separate part of yourself. It is actually grown and nurtured in the gap. This separate self is called *the will*. And when you place your will inside the gap and stay inside the gap, the will glows incandescently and grows stronger and stronger, until eventually you develop full illumination, full self-sovereignty. You become wilful and self-controlled. The will can't be developed anywhere else other than in that gap. And when you place your will between desire and inertia you form a triune, and create a brand new power that none of the three can generate alone.

Emerson's light bulb

It works very much like a light bulb that connects positive and negative (AC/DC) electrical currents by an element, exciting an arc of electricity to jump between the two poles, causing the element to glow red-hot and become incandescent. It's by connecting the positive and the negative with the element that light is produced. Early experiments in trying to make the electric light a sustainable form of illumination were hampered by the fact that oxidation caused the connecting element to burn out very quickly after the arc of light was created. Emerson discovered that if he could create a vacuum around the element, using a small glass bulb and a candle to burn up all the existing oxygen, the element would burn for a very long period of time. In discovering this he created the electric light bulb, a means of sustainable lighting that is still being used today by billions of people around the world. In our analogy, the AC/DC would be represented by desire (positive current) and inertia (negative current), with the will acting as the connecting element that excites the arc of light. Without the connecting element of will there can be no light. In our case, oxidation occurs when we fail to create a vacuum around ourselves, and so our initial impulse, our element (or in this case our will) is quickly extinguished by the excessive oxygen of other people's impressions.

Let me give you an example: You have a great business idea (desire) that creates a lot of internal excitement. This energy is used to fuel your will, which you place between the opposing currents of inertia and desire. This creates a bright incandescent light. But, very shortly after the initial connection, you allow your element to be burned out by the opinions you hear on the news, in the papers, from your friends or loved ones, and suddenly what started out as a bright light with a lot of life ends up burning out and you have to start all over again. The element (the will) can also burn out if we oxidise it by giving it too much attention too soon. I have lost count of the number of people I see who decide to do something, start a martial arts club for instance, buy all the gear (all the gear, no idea), go at it night and day for a few weeks and then literally burn themselves out. This is the same with hobbies, with businesses and often even with new partners.

To keep the element or the will hot and incandescent, you need protection from yourself and from others. You do this by creating a vacuum around yourself that prevents the oxidation caused by your own overzealousness and by other people's negativity. One of my friends decided to become a great judo player; he was so enthusiastic that he bought three judo suits so that he could train every day, he bought all the books and all the instructional tapes and he paid a small fortune for world-class private instruction. For the first month he was flying and his level of ability rose dramatically but by the second month he was already flagging, his body was cracking under the strain and his enthusiasm was waning. By the third month he'd given up completely; he was burned out. His will was oxidised by gross overexposure, the classic 'too much too soon'.

I once overcame the inertia to write a novel by creating a lot of internal excitement, only to find my will and enthusiasm oxidised 75,000 words in by the negativity of my then literary agent, ironically someone that I should have been able to trust. She initially loved my idea, but later said that she thought it didn't have legs because she'd shown it to other people and they didn't get it. I'd created a great energy to write this book, and placed a vacuum around me to protect it by keeping the project as private as possible, not talking to anyone about it, and certainly not sharing the chapters or the concepts with other people. But I let my guard down at the last minute, and I allowed negative oxygen to enter the vacuum. I sent some of the unfinished chapters to the lady in question and I asked her opinion of the novel so far, knowing instinctively that this is rarely a good idea, because the words and the concepts and the characters are still forming on the page at this stage and are easily damaged or killed by thoughtless criticism. Her negative response to the work added great power to an inertia that was already trying to break into my routine. My desire was oxidised and I never finished the book. I learned a massive lesson from this: once you start the work, never let up momentum and keep a tight vacuum around you at all times. And don't try to build your Rome in one day, because you will just burn out.

Good, positive information dissolves negativity, and it also helps to build your desire to the point where it outweighs inertia and triggers the will to act.

Once the embers of your desire are glowing, don't blow them too hard, too fast or too frequently or the flame you are trying to excite will be puffed out.

Negative information dissolves will, and disables you. That's why the vacuum is imperative.

Growing the will

Once the will acts, it is already in the process of growing. And, as I said earlier, it is not your willpower that grows, it is a separate you (called here 'the will') that is born, a separate and unique you that, if nurtured and exercised, will squeeze out and dissolve negativity until all that's left is pure unadulterated will. There can be no room in you for shadows when you have an all-powerful will.

Your true self is born and fed and nurtured to full maturity in this gap.

With this in mind I try to open as many inlets for light as possible – empowering information in all its forms: heard, seen, smelt, touched – and as many outlets for my negativity as I can find: physical (massage, exercise), psychological (counselling, therapy, writing, art, etc.), physiological (breathing, yoga) and spiritual (meditation, prayer, focus). More on this in a later chapter.

The power lies within us to become self-reliant, to take control of our lives by being pre-emptive and helping ourselves. No longer are we treading lightly and quietly through life in the hope that perhaps we will go unnoticed and un-criticised; instead we are donning our courage armour and going into battle with our elementary fears.

Now is a time for heroes, and heroes are men and women of action; they always place their bones between desire and inertia and create great light.

And light dissolves shadow.

And understanding shadow is what I'd like to look at next.

Chapter 3

Understanding Shadow

In this chapter I'd like to explore in more detail the nature of shadow, so that you can better recognise and ultimately release yourself from it. The main categories of shadow that we will explore are: **historical** (a negative belief that we learned as children and have subsequently carried into adult life, or emotional pain, trapped inside us by a past trauma); **current** (the things we face on a daily basis); **future** (our fear of what the future might bring); **borrowed** (fears that others implant in us if we do not properly protect ourselves); and the **bling** shadow, a false self who believes that freedom lies in material success. There are also sub-categories of shadow that we can examine en route.

It's interesting, actually, that as I write these words I find myself facing and dissolving the last remnants of one of my own long-established shadows, a sub-personality that has haunted me for as long as I can remember, one that I deliberately lured out into the open in a bid to dissolve it.

I recently released my first feature film, *Clubbed*, into the cinemas and so you'd think I'd be overjoyed. I should have been celebrating. I should have been throwing parties and screaming from the rooftops, 'Come one and come all to celebrate our achievement!' Writing a film, getting it made, seeing it in the cinemas and reviewed and talked about in national newspapers and on TV is what I had always dreamed about. But once it had happened and my dream had become manifest I felt... well, I felt scared, terrified actually (or, should I say, a small part of me felt terrified). I was trying to find a better word, one that might sound less wimpish, but terrified best describes how I felt. Not frightened of being hurt, not scared of physical confrontation and not even afraid of dying. My fear was of being criticised. This shadow (that was sat bubbling and churning in my belly) was exactly and unequivocally why I stuck my head above the parapet in the first place. I wanted to draw it out into the open so that I could finally free myself of this debilitating fear, and the only way I could do that was to actually place myself into a situation that triggered it. We had very mixed reviews of the film, a polarity of opinion that ranged from the very dire and upsetting *worst film of the year* to the wonderful and uplifting *the new Clockwork Orange!* Some of the polarity actually came from different people within the same newspaper: the *Sun* called it the new *Trainspotting* and its sister paper the *News of the World* gave it one star. *The Times* also gave us one star, while *The Sunday Times* said that British film has never been so good.

It's clear that criticism is just one man's opinion, and as such should hold no significance, but despite this worthy philosophical axiom, the savagery of the worst critique did strike terror in me, simply because it triggered the shadow part of me that was terrified of the negative opinion of others. Even as I am writing this I feel silly. What a ridiculous thing. Someone's opinion striking terror! It is hardly life and death; there is no maniac on the loose with a gun and a contract containing my personal details and instructions to shoot on sight! No one is trying to kill me. But… for some reason, the savage criticism did feel like this.

During the worst of the criticism, when my scared shadow emerged, I did (I confess) consider taking the 'flight' option and buying a teashop near the sea, away from it all. Only my massive experience in things confrontational enabled me to sit in the middle of the fear and recognise that it was not me who was scared. Rather, it was a sub-personality (my shadow) and I was finally able to laugh at how illusory the whole thing was and at how impotent criticism is when you look at it in its true light.

But the only way I was able to overcome my fear of being criticised and dissolve the shadow was to bring it into the light (everything that is exposed to light itself becomes light – more on this in later chapters). So I deliberately produced a piece of work (my film) that I knew would draw a heavy polarity of opinion, and when my shadow (my frightened self) emerged from flesh and urged me to find a safe haven, to hide or to run for my very life (such is the power of terror) I did none of the above. Instead, I faced the fear head on. I sat in the fear, I observed the people criticising me and I observed the shadow part of me that felt threatened by their criticism and I marinated. And when I did, very gradually, the shadow dissipated.

During the worst period, when I was actually in the eye of the storm, I remember smiling to myself and thinking, Is this it? Because if this is all you've got, bring it on, I can deal with this all day long. What I had thought might be a three-dimensional monster actually turned out to be (when faced) a two-dimensional cartoon that was about as deadly as a plastic spider. What I realised and what I learned from this encounter is that shadow is ephemeral, a harmless apparition that has no substance outside of unschooled imagination. And once I understood this, once I really got it, I felt encouraged to take on all of my demons, and prove that none of them have any existence. When you stop imagining monsters, monsters disappear.

The irony is that you have to approach and face these shadows before this truth becomes evident. From a distance they do look very real, and each time you're faced with a situation that triggers your shadow and your anticipation goes to work you get fooled once again into thinking, This one is real; this one is potent. In fact, you get fooled into thinking that this shadow is you! But it is not you, certainly not the living flowing vibrant you; rather, it is a just an old shadow of you that temporarily looks through your eyes.

None of your shadows are the real you.

Shadow disguises

Shadows take many forms and come in many different disguises. Your shadow might not be a fear of criticism, though. It might be a jealousy shadow, or it could be an envy shadow or perhaps a sub-personality that feels greed, lust, anger or sloth (or any of the seven deadly sins). You may be mildly conscious of your shadows; perhaps they are bubbling just below the surface. You may possibly be patently aware of them but for some reason can't face them down, or your shadows might be suppressed to the level of vague knowing, even repressed so deeply that you are completely unaware of them. You may even have given your shadow a different name so that you don't have to look at it. When I was younger and had an unhealthy fear of competitive sport, I could never admit my fear, not even to myself, because admitting it felt weak. Instead I told myself and anyone else who would listen: 'I am not afraid of it, I just don't want to do it. It's not me.' This is a bit like saying, 'I could give up cigarettes any time I want to, I just don't want to.' The greatest strength and the biggest courage is in first admitting to yourself that you are afraid (or that you have shadows that are afraid); the next courage comes in doing something about it.

Once you've acknowledged a shadow, it's already exposed to the light of your conscious mind. Generally, whether the shadow is bubbling just below the veneer or buried deep below layers of consciousness, we tend to do nothing about them. Usually we don't even acknowledge their existence; we just drag ourselves through life with the shadows hanging from and feeding off us like vultures. Until, that is, a life situation jars them into consciousness and we feel their effects in our body and mind.

What is shadow?

The psychiatrist Carl Jung thought of the shadow as unexpressed, perhaps trapped emotion; the psychologist Sigmund Freud linked them to sexual tensions that had no physical outlet; the spiritual teacher Eckhart Tolle calls the shadow a 'pain body' and describes it as old parts of the self trapped and imprisoned inside us, always looking for release, but at the same time always fearing release. The Christian Bible suggests that shadows are sins or errors that need the absolution of Christ (when our sins are absolved we become one again with God). Paramahansa Yogananda, one of the most pre-eminent spiritual figures of our time and founder of the Self-Realization Fellowship, suggested that some shadows are 'tramp souls', the demonic and disembodied souls that break into our mortal coil like squatters and live vicariously off and through us. G. I. Gurdjieff believed that shadows are sub-personalities and that we all have thousands of them, each taking their turn to control our body (usually unconsciously, often against our best instincts), keeping our true self asleep with their busy smokescreen illusions. He believed, as I believe, that we have many incongruous personalities sharing the same body, usually without one true leader, like a pack of mutts without a top dog. We are at once Christian and atheist (today we happily give alms to the poor and needy; tomorrow we attack the poor and needy for being lazy ingrates). We are moral and we are immoral or amoral (we talk publicly of integrity, while in private we fiddle our taxes; we claim that we are not concerned with morals, and yet we attack other people for being immoral). We are loyal and yet we are deeply unfaithful (outwardly we boast fidelity, but we are disloyal in our thoughts and in our deeds). We are puritans and yet we are purveyors of vice (we preach but we do not practise what we preach). We are non-judgemental and we are hypercritical (we gossip and judge others and then kid ourselves that our gossip and judgement is objective and compassionate by using a weak, rationalised preface to our scandal, such as 'I really like him but…'). In essence very few people are congruent; very few people are unified, absolute or One. We are at once many disparate characters, with various different, contradictory personalities that are often warring inside of us like opposing armies at the battle of Kuruksetra (an epic war depicted in the spiritual classic *The Bagahavad Gita*), each fighting for sovereignty over the body.

The absolute

The purpose of this information is to help the reader to first recognise and then clear all the sub-personalities or shadows that are not true, and to help to bring unity. If we don't become absolute we're always going to be driven to distraction by the strongest dog inside us (the one we feed the most), who'll get us into all sorts of trouble, against our will. You've probably heard it a million times: someone acts inappropriately and gets into trouble, then afterwards, bemused and shocked by their own actions says, 'I don't know what came over me. That was not me!' While it perhaps was not their usual or even their best self, it is certainly one of their selves. And that self, that shadow, that sub-personality might end up putting them in a divorce court, a prison cell or even a hospital morgue.

Your disloyal shadow has an affair with the girl at work and leaves you to pick up the pieces. Your dishonest shadow lies and steals, leaving you with a court case and the charge of losing your integrity. Your greedy shadow eats and drinks and indulges to excess, leaving you to pay the price with obesity and poor health. They are all in you, even if you think they're not. Observe yourself over a day or over a week and see how many times you 'step out of character', and see how many different personalities come forward that are not the real you. See how many of these personalities you actually don't like or respect or are ashamed of: the angry character that rages violently on the road (a 'usually very nice' woman recently threatened to 'fucking bastard kill' my friend, a delivery driver, when he blocked the traffic for a few minutes to unload a chair from his van); the greedy character that is always ravenous and envious for more than they currently have; the creepy sycophant who climbs the social ladder just to get ahead, even when it means working with unsavoury or dishonest people (other people's shadows); the shadow that lustfully ogles their friend's wife and even has sex with her in his mind's eye when he is making love to his own wife; or the envious shadow that throws their ugly vitriol at the TV screen when a presenter or a personality comes on that they particularly dislike.

The key is to recognise these separate personalities and work towards dissolving them until all that's left is the real you. And you'll know your true self easily enough; he or she is the one that is altruistic, gentle, patient, honest, thoughtful, generous, charitable, forgiving, philanthropic and loving. This is the self that you need to develop; this is your top dog. And you develop it by identifying and bringing it to the forefront, feeding and encouraging your top dog. At the same time you also need to recognise (and this is hard, because people will deny separate personalities all day long) all the other shadowy impostors, the hijackers and the squatters, and stop feeding them. You must be brutal with this. If you are in denial, or if you flirt with these shadows, you'll be in trouble.

The denial shadow

Shadow can be very subtle. An honest man who doesn't acknowledge any trace of dishonesty in himself (he is in denial) gets into big trouble with the police after buying a stolen flat-screen TV from the back of a lorry. Up until that point he'd rationalised his dishonesty by convincing himself that buying stolen gear is not the same as going into a shop and stealing it, kidding himself that because 'these big stores are all heavily insured' no one gets hurt, so it's alright!

A loyal spouse in denial of their low self-esteem will be easily seduced into an affair through flattery. I have a very handsome friend who has just destroyed his marriage and shattered his integrity by giving his fidelity away to the lowest bidder. Although he's very handsome, he has a low self-worth shadow that he doesn't acknowledge. It's clearly there because, even though he has a beautiful and loyal wife, he keeps flirting with other women. He claims (like many men) that he's just window shopping and that 'as long as I don't go in and buy it's OK'. What he's really doing is lying to himself and feeding his insecurity shadow. His marriage failed (and he is desperate to get his wife back, but she is not having any of it) after he was flattered and seduced by a girl who could not be uglier if she had three heads. Ultimately it was not his shadow that got him into trouble; it was the denial of his shadow. Because he didn't acknowledge it, it was given free rein. You must recognise it, and once accepted you must start the eviction process.

Inside you there is an observer, your true self, the part of you that knows, and that is aware of what is occurring. And it is this very awareness that grows your true self. Understanding and identifying this process is imperative. You can't work on something if you do not acknowledge its existence.

You can call the shadow *trapped energy*, *internal demons*, *pain bodies* or *multiple personalities*; the name doesn't matter too much. What is important is how the shadows affect you in the here and now, and ultimately how they stop you from moving forward into a bright new tomorrow and living the life you deserve and were born to live.

We must not allow our shadows to keep us home like a jealous spouse; nor should we sit behind the twitching curtains of everyday life waiting for the assault of our fears. Rather, we should go out like warriors into the night and hunt our demons down. Why wait to be attacked when we can attack pre-emptively? It is nobler and certainly more empowering to take the initiative and lead an assault. Shakespeare suggested as much when he wrote (in *Hamlet*), 'whether 'tis nobler in the mind to suffer the slings and arrows of outrageous fortune, or take arms against a sea of troubles, and by opposing, end them'. My instinct and my experience tells me that it is righteous, it is character-building and it is cleansing to muster up the courage, take arms and clear yourself of all personalities that do not serve you.

We can do this in several different ways, all of which I will talk about later in the book, in greater detail.

It'll be useful at this stage to go through the different types of shadow, so that you can better understand and therefore recognise and dissolve them, starting with the most prominent of them all, the historical shadow.

Historical shadow

Most shadows are historical. That is, they're learned fears: things that we were taught or things that we experienced as we grew up. I would say that, from my own experience, historical shadows are the worst offenders and are nearly always responsible for our present angst. When we fear to move towards a better life it's the historical shadow that blocks our path. Because we're so used to living with historical shadows we rarely question or even recognise them. They will usually present themselves in the form of a negative voice (or voices) that tries to dissuade us from moving house, changing job, travelling the world, etc. And to make sure that we hear and heed them we will usually get a drop of adrenalin (even terror or depression) that forces us back to the centre of our present existence. Any change in the norm will threaten the comfort of the historical shadow, and when it does it will let us know. And if the shift is major, like a radical change in career or location or partner, it will often create havoc, because major life changes don't only threaten the comfort of shadow (and they do like to feed on comfort), they also threaten the actual existence of it.

When I was a nine-to-five factory worker and I wanted to be a nightclub bouncer (becoming a nightclub bouncer was part of my early shadow-hunting campaign; I had a fear of violent confrontation, so I became a bouncer to dissolve my fear) my shadow triggered huge amounts of anxiety, my body was flooded with adrenalin and everything inside me wanted to run. Becoming a bouncer was way, way outside of my usual orbit, and to become a man of the doors, to risk life and limb, I would have to create a whole new reality and forge a whole new identity. So becoming a bouncer was not just a change of job, it was actually a full-on change of character. It meant eliminating one of my major sub-personalities. My historical shadow was the inbuilt lesson I'd been schooled in since I was a baby. It was the *shadow of pretension*. I was weaned on living a good life, but an ordinary life; I was taught to be a nice person, but not one that tried to stand out; I was schooled in the art of mediocrity, and any ambition outside of the norm was seen as pretentious. Even if I talked about ambition, it was quickly shot down by other folk tuning into the same frequency who told me not to get above my station. And if I ever moved towards greener pastures I was warned and forewarned of the inherent dangers of stepping outside the known, often even threatened. One lady that I loved for a long time was so unbalanced by my ambition to be a great martial artist that she forced me to choose: 'Me or the judo,' she said. Well, I'd already brought the suit, so... she had to go! In this instance, as in many similar instances, my ambition triggered her shadow, and it was her shadow (as opposed to her) that tried to block my path. If she'd been braver, or a little more enlightened, she might have used the situation to dissolve one of her own fears, and we could have grown together. If I'd have been more knowledgeable about this process I might have been able to help her.

The angst and the terror exist because the discomfort triggered by change gives birth to a new identity, but this also means the death, or certainly the transition, of the old identity (or the shadow). The part of me that was terrified of violent confrontation didn't want me to become a bouncer, it felt too threatened by that, so it made its position known and clear by triggering copious amounts of adrenalin. When that didn't work, and it became very obvious that I was going to make the change no matter what, my body and my mind became inhospitable for that particular shadow. So it jumped ship. It left the building. A new *me* was born, and with that new courageous me came a widening perspective. My belief system expanded; suddenly I found myself thinking, Wow! If I can be a bouncer in some of the toughest clubs in Britain, what else could I do? After successfully working in one of the most violent employs known to man, I felt as though there was nothing I couldn't achieve. The sky was way below my limit now, my burgeoning will suddenly had sinewy muscles, and even the constellations were getting out of my way in case I set my sights on the stars. Of course, this was not without its difficulties; it took me ten years of working as a bouncer to forge the new me and finally dissolve the old. It didn't happen overnight, and I had many scary situations thrust upon me before I was fully formed and ready to take my new identity even further (see my book *Watch My Back*).

Thankfully, by the time I left the safety of factory work for the beer and blood of door security I was already quite the seasoned shadow hunter, and was able to override the fear that frightened me more than the four horsemen of the apocalypse.

So fear of violent confrontation was a historical (and quite a natural) fear. For most people the fear of violence stays natural. If there is a confrontation in their immediate vicinity, they react as nature intended and they either fight or they run. For me, however, being very sympathetic sensitive (very sensitive to stress), the fear of violent confrontation was actually debilitating. It affected my whole life. In fact, by the time I'd reached my mid-twenties, I went through periods of feeling pretty much frightened of everything. By then I was a black belt in karate, I was a shift worker in a factory, I had a wife and (at the time) three great kids (I now have four great kids) and I was living an ordinary life. You wouldn't have looked at me and immediately recognised a fearful man. Quite the contrary. At times I was confident and articulate, and other than the fact that I was very, very driven and had massive (as yet unrealised) ambitions beyond working in the factory, I was quite normal. It was only when my norm was threatened that things became debilitating.

For instance, I mentioned above that I worked shifts in a chemical factory. What I didn't mention was the fact that, while it paid my bills and I was grateful for that, I hated working in a chemical factory only marginally less than I hated working shifts, and that hate was on a par with the hate of having a body part ripped off in a spinning lathe. I hated it and talked incessantly about leaving it, but… I was too scared to actually do it. When I thought about a better life I got excited. The idea was splendid enough, let me tell you. It was an idea worth celebrating. However, the moment I took the idea and tried to run with it, tried to actually place it into action, a myriad different things rose up *inside and out* that dragged me back to the centre of simple and the norm. My partner ('Why can't you be happy where you are?'), my workmates ('It's not safe out there – jobs like this don't grow on trees.'), even my environment seemed to be screaming at me, 'Who do you think you are?' I can see now, with the great benefit of hindsight, that all these things were little more than excuses that my historical shadow had projected and used to keep me exactly where I was. And once I realised this, once I understood that if I was to become the man I knew I could be I had to lose this cowardly shadow, it left me quicker than a greyhound in the back seat of a Porsche 911.

Current shadow

The world is changing all around us, all the time. Of that there can be no doubt. In fact, change is the only constant. It's the one thing that you can always rely on. One of our great problems as a species is that we don't deal with change very well. We don't embrace it; in fact we fear change, and actively resist or even attack it. This, of course, is an act of folly, like a piece of balsa wood trying to resist the ocean.

We are today a product of what we did yesterday, and we will be tomorrow what we do today, so most of our current angst is a result of historical shadow. And historical shadow is often so deeply embedded in our psyche that we hardly notice it's there any more. We may have an underlying feeling of anger, of unhappiness or frustration, but we often don't quite know what to associate it with. A closer examination usually reveals to us that we're not living authentic lives, and we are not living authentically because of old beliefs or old scars. One of my current shadows before I became a full-time martial arts instructor many years ago was a very strong belief that teaching martial arts was not a realistic ambition (that is what I had been told), and that somehow it was not a 'proper' job; 'people like us' were supposed to fill the factories and work in menial employment. I'd like to tell you that this was just an innate belief, or one that was intuited, but actually it was much more sinister than that. All my parents' generation knew was hard, manual, often menial work and gratitude. If you had a job you were grateful to be placing bread on the table and you neither argued with that nor did you aspire to anything better; if you did you certainly didn't voice your aspiration. Those brave enough to announce their ambitions were often looked down upon and seen as being up their own rear orifice or, that delicious old saying, 'above their station'. We were weaned on limitation, and if we aspired to a path outside of limitation we were accused of being greedy and ungrateful. I remember talking about this with a couple of friends. I was telling them about the importance of teaching children that anything is possible, and that if heady ambition was married with a strong work ethic and escalating instruction there could be no limitations. The woman agreed effusively and told me how she always inspired her teenage son with the belief that he could be anything he wanted to be. 'Except be a professional footballer of course!' Her husband chipped in as a caveat. 'Oh yes,' she concurred, 'he can't be a professional footballer! We soon knocked that silly notion out of his head. I mean the odds of becoming a professional footballer…'

Like most people, they had limiting beliefs or shadows, and they didn't just pass those beliefs onto their son (installing and maintaining a strong current shadow), they pumped them directly into his veins. What I had to learn – and this was hard because it meant going against every instinct I had – was that the people we love, even and especially those closest to us, are not always right! They can only teach us what they know, and often what they know is not true, or certainly it's very limited. It was perhaps true for them, because truth is the sum of a person's knowing, but it was not my truth. This became evident for me, and it was a revelation, when I got my first book published in 1992. Up until that point my current shadow (informed by what I was being told every single day of my life) told me constantly that it was nigh on impossible to become a published author; the odds were so small that apparently they didn't even attract official odds. My shadow was strong because it was not just what I'd been taught (my historical shadow), it was what I was still being told (my current shadow) every day and I could see no direct evidence in my immediate milieu of anything to contradict this schooling – I didn't know a single person who'd had a book published. And although I could see a possibility-light at the very end of a dark tunnel, it was distant and it was faint. And every time I got a knock-back from a publisher ('leave your number in the bin'), that light seemed to get dimmer and dimmer. For some people the current shadow is so strong that they never actually sit down to write their opus in the first place because their shadow says, 'What's the point? Who's going to publish me?' And the collective shadow all around them concurs.

Writing down my initial shadow inventory (I called it my fear pyramid back then) and clearing lots of historical fears expanded my belief system; like climbing a high mountain and looking out, it gave me a greater perspective. Lots of the things that I'd been taught as being true turned out to be someone else's truth and not mine. This shattering of old beliefs gave me a lot of courage and a brand new viewpoint. If (I remember thinking) I can become a doorman – a life-threatening employ – if I can become a full-time martial arts instructor – and everyone said that I could never make a living doing that – then what else could I do, and what else was a lie? Why couldn't I write a book? When I finally got my first acceptance letter from Summersdale Publishers for a book I penned called *Watch My Back*, it was like the world suddenly opened up for me. The belief that people like me do not become writers was so strong that, when I shattered it by proving it to be wrong, it challenged everything I had ever learned about the world. It was as though I was suddenly rocketed into a brand new reality where everything really was possible, where you really could do anything you wanted to do. If I could publish one book, why not two? Why not three? (I am currently up to about forty books.) And if I could publish a book and get paid for it what was there to stop me from becoming a full-time writer? What was there to stop me from writing journalism, instructional books, stage plays and films?

Fucking nothing was the answer.

Clearing that one single shadow transformed my entire existence. I've since gone on to do all those things and more. And I've gone onto do them because suddenly I knew I could, but only after I gave myself a clear vision by challenging my current shadow, and that was only possible because I cleared the way by dissolving that shadow.

Manually change the current information that you are receiving and you will begin to change and dissolve the current shadow.

Borrowed shadow

Have you ever woken in the morning and thought, Today I'm going to change the world! only to find after five minutes talking to a negative spouse or a derogatory family member or friend that you no longer feel inspired enough to change your pants? Have you ever had a great idea for a new business, or a story or a piece of art that has been shot out of the sky by a friend or a colleague who felt it their duty to 'manage your expectations' (a 'flavour expression' used by people with small imaginations that really want to say, 'For fuck's sake, who do you think you are? Be realistic!') and show you the shortfalls of your innovation, or drown you with waves of information about the economic climate and why now is a time for safety not silly notions and dreams? And do you find yourself wading though days of melancholy waiting and praying for the next holiday, because everyone around you is also wading through days of melancholy, waiting and praying for their next holiday?

If you do, you have almost certainly borrowed a shadow. And if you borrow a shadow, even if you only adopt it on for a minute or an hour, you become that shadow. And people are always inadvertently shoving their shadows onto you and anyone else who leaves themselves unprotected. We tend to wander though life like a carriage without a directing passenger, allowing anyone and everyone to jump in the back seat and direct us to their destination of choice, normally somewhere dark and dire, certainly not a destination of our own choosing. This happens mostly because we're unaware of the fact that we have shadow, and that others have shadow and that their shadow can and will and does affect us in a very real way. When you leave the company of someone and you feel negative about your day or pessimistic about your life, you are borrowing shadow; if you watch a TV programme and feel uninspired or depressed, you are borrowing shadow; if you pick up a newspaper and reading it makes you feel as though there is no future, you are not only borrowing shadow, you are allowing an individual shadow (from one person) or a collective shadow (from the general consensus) to direct your life. To be happy, to be fulfilled, to be successful, you have to become top dog in your own body; you have to take command of your own internal shadows and either drive them to work ('giving your vices voices' – more on this later) because they can be a rich source of energy, or if they are destructive drive them out, by taking yourself to an altitude that they can't survive at. And certainly you have to be very careful of the company you keep and protect yourself against the invasion of foreign shadows. Being careful about the company you keep is easy enough in theory: just change the company you keep. You don't necessarily need to make a huge announcement about this, just gradually pull away from negative influences and swap them for better ones. And defending yourself against the shadows of other people means literally that: if they attack you, if they try to pull you down, if they try to dismantle your dreams and fill you with negativity, defend yourself, fight for your ideas, protect your dreams and block negativity by underlining your own beliefs. When someone tells you that the current climate will not support your ideas, tell them that you disagree and that good ideas will grow in any climate. If they tell you that the world is dark, tell them that your world is full of light. In fact, it's easier than that. If you keep getting negative comments from your friends, change your friends.

Old shadow friends

I was recently forced to do exactly this, at an old friend's fiftieth birthday party. The night started well enough and I was delighted to see people that I hadn't seen for ages. One of my very old friends was there (let's call him Jim), a man I'd trained with in the past; we even fought together in America when we were over there with an English karate team fighting in the USA open championships. Since those days I've tightened my internal game considerably, I have renounced violence and eschewed old and redundant ways, and I've also abstained from alcohol in my bid to oust shadows and in my search for self-sovereignty. I make (and on the night I made) no big announcement about this; it does nothing but get people's backs up because when you broadcast your positive intentions they tend to think you're titling a lance at them. But when you're in a room full of heavy drinkers, the fact that you're drinking Diet Coke and not talking-out-of-your-arse drunk (like everyone else) soon becomes apparent. And with every drink that my friend Jim threw past his tonsils he seemed to notice more and more that I was not drinking. In all honesty, I'd not noticed that he had noticed. I was just busy chatting away with old friends. That is, until Jim stood in front of me. His mind was addled with the drink, his mouth was twisted with derision and he asked me, 'Who do you think you are?' I was a bit taken aback to be honest, because I like Jim. I knew that he had problems with drink and drugs and sexual pornography; I knew that, as my life had lifted because of my commitment to shadow hunting, his had taken a downward turn because he had become his addictions. But I didn't judge him. I don't judge; I've made too many mistakes myself in the past to judge any man, and his life was his choice and nothing to do with me.

Who did I think I was?

That's what he asked. He was very aggressive with his question, quite challenging, and he was a lump, a former doorman and a strong fighter so his presence in front of me was very real. I asked him what he meant, and he reeled out a diatribe of abuse about me not drinking and me not taking drugs and me thinking that I was something special. He was obviously offended by my life choices; he even suggested that my clean living was an attempt at trying to live for ever, and then he assured me of the fact that I would be in the grave long before him. He was right on two points: I do know I'm going to live for ever, although there will be no specific attempt to do so – I understand enough about science to know that nothing can die, only transform – and I have enough faith in God to trust that there is a life, hereafter. And yes, he also had me on the 'something special' point. I have to admit that I do think I'm something special. But then I think everyone is something special; in fact, the longer I live on this beautiful blue marble the more I'm convinced this is true. So I tried to explain to Jim that my choices were my own and that I was just trying to live the best life I could in the best way I knew how. When his aggression escalated and he started to square up to me, I quickly realised that my presence, my light, was an offence, not to my old mate Jim, but to the many shadows that he was harbouring. And let me be very clear of one thing here: I do not tolerate shadows, especially when they bloat their chest in front of me and posture. I understood that his diatribe was an attempt to attack my life and my beliefs and force his shadow into me. And it was then I realised that I needed to defend myself. I squared him up, I looked him in the eye and I told him why I loved the life I lived and why I made the choices I had made: basically because I intended to be an individual and I didn't want to end up living a reheated, microwave-dinner of an existence like him, a sheep, the slave of his addictions. The moment I let loose his shadow retreated and my old mate Jim emerged with a sorry look on his face and a throat full of sad pathetic apology. His head slumped, his demeanour collapsed and he started to tell me how shit his life was, how he wished he could be like me and that he so genuinely wanted to be an individual, but... he just couldn't let go of his vices.

This is and this was an example of borrowed shadow and how to defend yourself against the shadows of others (more on this later).

In order to fight your own corner you need to really believe in yourself. You have to have faith in your path and trust in your philosophy. Otherwise you'll end up like everyone else, leaning on the bar, talking shit, and living a lie.

The bling shadow

To conclude this chapter I'd like to look at some of the external distractions that we often don't recognise as shadow. They're what I call (collectively) 'the bling shadow', the materialistic lure that often keeps us stuck to the wheel of Maya (illusion). It is the great seducer of man, and has been since time began, and all great thinkers throughout history agree that this is the greatest illusion of them all. The illusion is power, in the form of *fame, fortune and honours*. We search for them, more often than not in vain, because we think that the acquisition of one (or of all) will bring us the ultimate elixir: happiness. In and of themselves, this poisonous triune has no true power, they are all temporary, they are all ephemeral, and of this there can be no doubt. Take your wealth to a place that doesn't recognise the currency and it'll buy you nothing but misery; peddle your honours in a country where they're not recognised and the power you thought they brought will hold no sway. And all fame is local: in one city you may be revered, but in countless others you will be anonymous. Even global fame is but a speck of dust when compared to the constellations.

Fame can often become a prison; money brings the need for protection. And honours are like a yoke on your time and energy and a feedbag for your ego. Juvenal, a Roman poet, author of *The Satires* and thought to be the originator of the genre of Roman satire once said, 'the empty-handed traveller whistles when he passes the highwayman'. Note that these things in and of themselves can't be useful; we can and I think we must, do great things with our material gifts if we have them, but don't look to them as the harbinger of happiness because you will be disappointed. History and personal experience are proof enough of this. All of these impostors can be taken away from you by the fates, at any time, and if all your power is invested in what is effectively worthless ostentation, then you will always be at the mercy of chance. The carrot of fame, fortune and honours that life dangles before us promises much but delivers little. If they bring power it is temporal, if they give pleasure it is ephemeral and if they offer happiness it is only on loan, and may be recalled at anytime, without appointment and without permission. And this is the reason why I think everyone with a penchant for fame, fortune and honour should seek it out and they should seek it out now. As the prophet Osho said, 'You can see God better from a Rolls-Royce'. I think everyone who wants a Roller should have one, and those who seek celebrity should be given it, and money in abundance should be heaped upon those that think it has potency, because often it is not until you get it that you actually realise how transient it all is. When the Beatles were at the very peak of their fame they thought they had it all: celebrity, beautiful women and more money than they knew what to do with. But none of the fabulous four were happy, because in acquiring everything they lost more, and they all realised just how little they had. It was at this point that their spiritual search began. Similarly, we see people on the TV every day looking for the new panacea that is celebrity, and when they get it they are often disappointed or even destroyed by it, or their high counterbalances and they find themselves no happier than they were before, and so the search for more begins again. The D-list celebrities want to be C-list celebrities, and the C-list celebrities want to be B-list, and everyone, it would seem, wants to be an A-list celebrity. Those who earn a million want to earn ten million, and those that hit ten feel small compared to the conglomerates with a turnover of a billion, and even they squirm in the shadow of the multi-billionaire companies that could swallow them up like an appetiser. For those seeking fame, fortune and honours, there will never be enough to satiate their hunger. And each stage of the illusion brings more misery than the last, and promises that satiety and happiness are just around the next bend. Like Godot, it never seems to appear. At the same time, those with insatiable appetites live in fear of the wheel turning and taking back everything they have gained. So much so that we see a daily parade of yesterday's celebrities pulling humiliating party tricks on reality television in a bid to regain their lost fame. This eternal chase for bling shadow often completely possesses people, to the point that they become lost in the illusion and blind to the way out.

The only virtue in chasing bling shadow is that (as the poet William Blake said) the road of excess often leads to the palace of wisdom. How do you know that bling has no potency if you've never had bling? How can you tell that celebrity is a false god if you've never been famous? And you may never know the temporal nature of honours if no one ever awards you any. The best way to know for sure is to be there and experience it, and then you'll know. It is hard to renounce what you have never had.

I meet fiscally successful people every single week, and I have yet to find one who has found happiness in their material success. The smarter ones, however, have used their accomplishments to help them find true happiness, which is inside. Take your multi-millionaire bones to a Caribbean beach and sit with it, and you'll find that even the sunny idyll and a rake of cash can't take the shadow out of you. All it does is fatten it up.

The power of virtue

There is one thing, though, that can't be taken away from you, not by any person, and not by any situation, and that is equanimity; if we can develop self-reliance, self-sovereignty, through difficult endeavour, through bravely hunting shadow, through the acquisition of learned and earned wisdom, we will realise – as the wealthy Roman politician Boethius discovered awaiting execution in prison for a crime he didn't commit, and as Victor Frankle (a survivor from the German concentration camps in World War Two who went on to write a seminal book about his experiences called *Man's Search for Meaning*) found during his heinous incarceration – that when you have equanimity, there is no such thing as bad luck; every happening is a divine happening and everything that happens to you is good. Who you are, your wisdom and your freedom to choose your own response to the fickle nature of circumstance can never be taken away. This makes you all powerful.

Seeing fame and fortune with its make-up off might be a little bit depressing; if these things are a lie, then what does that leave us? Well, first of all, becoming happy doesn't mean that you can't have any material possessions; it doesn't mean that you don't have the fame, the fortune and the accolades. A man with wisdom will bear whatever life proffers with magnanimity. All it means is that you don't look to these things for your source of happiness. In the *Tao Te Ching* Lau Tsu says (verse 81) that 'the master has no possessions', but among those no possessions he may have two houses, a fast car and a private library. It is not about not having it, it is about not letting it define or own or be you, because if you do who are you? And who will you be when your fortune is suddenly taken away again? You have to be able to walk unaided, without golden crutches, and then you will be powerful.

You can find true happiness and still enjoy the toys that come with being in this mortal coil. It is a case of being in it but not off it. So you can enjoy them, like a teenager might enjoy an alternative reality on his Xbox; just don't allow yourself to believe that it is real.

The kingdom of God

In the King James Bible (**Matthew 6:33**) it says that we should 'seek first the kingdom of God and his righteousness, and then all things will be given unto you'. It goes on to say that the kingdom of God is within. So why are we looking outside? What I've learned and what I know is this: the kingdom of God is in us, but the pathway is blocked by our shadows, and when we clear those shadows we reconnect with God, the collective unconscious, our greater potential. In clearing shadows we develop courage and wisdom and other great virtues, and these cannot be taken away, not by fire, nor famine nor world recession. I think this is really exciting, because when you shadow hunt, when you connect with God, and when you create this deep and wide base to work from, it's not just peace of mind and happiness (which are worthy enough on their own) that you discover, you also become a conduit for God, the distributor of a great metaphysical force. Once you are set at this *God frequency* you become like a universal magnet that draws towards you everything you need.

While you fall for the bling shadow and spend your days tracing maps and chasing treasure you will be led down one blind alley after another, and even if you do find a chest of gold, it will not bring the promise it held. But if you make the hunt an inside job, and if you can master yourself, you will find peace and happiness and all of those other trinkets will come with it. You will be so balanced and so connected that the treasures will be falling from the sky.

Chapter 4

Many Hats, One Origin

It is easy to start delving into your mind or into the world in the hunt for shadow and get confused and baffled, because there often seem to be so many. Sometimes it seems as though you just get rid of one shadow when another one appears, then another. It can be very demoralising when you think that there might be no end to the shadows that we harbour inside of us and out.

What I learned from my own journey is that there is not a multitude of shadows; even if it appears superficially that there are, in actuality there is only one. But it wears many hats. The shadow can wear an anger hat, or a greed hat, it can be disguised as envy or lust, it might wear a hat that says *abandonment* or *violence*, or perhaps a fear of success, or fear of failure, even a fear of living. But when you strip them back and render them bare, when you take away their cunning disguises, you find that there is only one origin. And that origin is energy. At the root of everything is energy; when you chop off the labels and rip away the cloak you are left with naked and very potent energy that we use – or often misuse – to create the 10,000 things (Lau Tsu's definition of the physical world). Those who don't find an outlet for their energy become root-bound, their power turns in on them and they slowly – sometimes very quickly and violently – implode. Once we realise this, once we understand that everything is just energy that our judgements and perceptions have shaped into shadows (like fear and lust, etc.), we can break those emotions back down to their component parts and regenerate them into fuel for our external goals.

How wonderful.

All you need to make this a reality is a suitable outlet – preferably a creative outlet – somewhere to channel all that angst.

Giving your vices voices

Let me tell you briefly where I find my release (I will go into this in more detail in Chapter 9, Dissolving the Shadow). I find it in creativity. I write every day; it's my passion and it's my job and I love it. It's through the writing (what I call writing from the coal face or giving my vices a voice) that I have brought many of my shadows to the light. I type my angst onto the screen. I've found that a shadow left to itself will feed off any and every vice. In fact, it will become vice. Many good people have become vice addicts because they failed to manage their shadows; some have ruined their lives by courting crime, others drugs and more still sexual pornography. But if you can captain the shadow and find a creative outlet for it, you can give a powerful voice to those vices, and in the process clear your shadow for good. Interestingly, when I want to write really urgent and powerful shadows out of me, the kind that would normally look to vice for sustenance, I have to use a pen and paper rather than the computer keyboard.

I recently wrote a stage play called *3 Sacks Full of Hats*, for a London theatre. It is about the death of my brother Ray from alcoholism. I'd been trying to write the play for ten years, but it would never come out; there were too many layers of shadow on top of it. It was only after I cleared the surface shadows with daily writing and diligent introspection and meditation and sinewy work in the corporal world that *3 Sacks* finally emerged. I was talking to my friend Titas at the Finborough Theatre in London and he asked me if I'd like to write a play for them. We were sat in the busy bar of the theatre having a tea, and I told him that I'd like to write about the last three days of my brother's life, the denial and the shame and the destructive nature of alcohol, and how hideous my brother's death was and how privileged I felt being the one he chose to see him through to the next room, but also how very angry I was that he chose this way to live and ultimately this way to die. Almost as soon as I opened my mouth to talk the tears gushed and the narrative of the play presented itself to me then and there in the bar of the theatre. It offered itself to me so urgently that later that night I got out my pen and pad and I began to write. The play that took ten years to emerge was written in one session. It came out of me like hot lava; it was rich and painful and beautiful. In one session ten years' worth of build-up and forty years of shadow (I wrote about things I'd been carrying since childhood) emerged.

Initially I got into writing simply because I loved writing. Later I chased a career in writing because I thought that it might bring me money and fame and honours. It brought me plenty of that (thank you very much), but on its own this would not have been enough. I get paid for writing, it's my job, but more than that it's my catharsis; it's my atonement.

I'm not saying that this is the only way to create potent art, or that people without difficult backgrounds cannot do so; what I am saying is that if this flood of emotional energy is there anyway, why not use it? Why not draw from that reservoir and create a great life for yourself? This is what I've managed to do, so why not you?

I was a man filled with rage and anger and lust and violence and fear (just energy with labels) that all found roots in my very difficult early life experiences. And for three long decades I allowed that shadow to rule me and make me either outwardly violent or inwardly depressed. I desperately wanted to find a creative outlet (actually any outlet) for these feelings, but at the time I knew neither what the feelings were (only that they felt uncontrollable and scary) nor what to do with them. When I felt inspired I worked myself into the ground and tried to create Rome in a single day, and when the depression caught me I ended up walking out of the doctors' surgery with tablets that were designed to place a blanket over my feelings so that I was living my life as if underwater. Once I learned to understand the feelings, the shadow, the fear, I placed a yoke on the energy and put it to work and it produced for me prolifically. But – and this is true to this day – if I go too long without bleeding that energy I start to get clogged again, I feel depressed, I feel angry, I feel lustful and jealous and I get very paranoid.

So if you are filled to bursting with anger because you were abandoned as a child, or because your first wife betrayed you, or because you were abused, or because you were brought up in a poor environment, good. Very good. Excellent. You have something there that you can work with. If you can develop the self-discipline to control these very strong emotions, strip away their labels and channel the energy that is left into something worthy, you are destined for success.

Shadow as identity

One of the common complaints I hear when I'm on my travels is people claiming that they're unable to make a success in their life because they had a terrible upbringing. But loads of very successful people had terrible upbringings; it didn't stop them. Others were abused as children and say that this has ruined their life and that's why they can't be a success. But we know that lots of people were abused and became a huge success anyway. Others say that they had no education, and they blame their parents, they blame their teachers, they blame the government, or anyone else that falls into their eyeline. But we know that there is a plethora of highly successful, very happy people who created their kingdoms from dust. Many of them were misdiagnosed dyslexics as kids so missed out on their education, others didn't even get offered an education, more still eschewed traditional schooling and went instead straight into the workplace and developed their business acumen on the shop floor.

I learned early on that having shit in your past will only stop you from moving forward if you want it to. With one decision (to use everything in your life as grist) your shit could become the raw material for an amazing and prolific future. This is not to say that people are not traumatised by their past, or that there is no merit in their pain – of course there is and it would be unkind to suggest otherwise. What I am saying is that with a strong will (and the will can always be developed in the power triune if you have one that is weak) you can do something about it. So if you have had it bad in the past, good; you can do something with that raw energy. You can use it to make gold. Stop complaining about how bad it was, because it doesn't help; stop feeling sorry for yourself because you are where you are. Complaining and marinating in self-pity only serves to keep you there. Don't make the same mistake as many and make an identity out of your pain; saying 'Poor little me' might get you a bit of short-term sympathy, but in the long run it will not get you a life, certainly not any kind of life that I would like to live.

I've tried all of the aforementioned and I've lived that sad life. When I realised that it was not a profitable way to exist I changed myself and I chose better. You can choose better too. When you allow your pain to become your identity you have allowed a shadow to become a host in your body. And while it is delicious being a martyr, it is fucking tiresome.

I have a friend who lost his wife to suicide. It was tragic. His wife seemed like an ordinary girl, and if she was depressed (and it turned out that she was very depressed) he didn't know about it. In fact, his wife managed to hide it from everyone until she killed herself and left a note saying that she no longer wanted to live, even though she had a doting husband and a beautiful daughter. It is very tragic and we all mourned her passing. Five years on my friend is still mourning. He teaches his child to mourn; he schools his friends in the art of mourning. His identity has become that of the mourning husband. He visits his wife's grave every day, and he relives her tragic passing from morning till night, telling his story to anyone that will listen. We all understand and can, I am sure, sympathise with his pain. It is an awful way to lose a loved one, but his wife is dead, and he won't let go. I saw him the other day for the first time in years, and all he wanted to talk about was how devastated he still is, how he has never taken another girlfriend, and how he never will and how he is just waiting to die so that he can be with his wife again. In the meantime he's like the walking dead. He is a martyr to his loss, wasting a life that others would definitely honour more. He's taken an opportunity to opt out of the race, believing that the death of his wife justifies this. Really, he's just scared to carry on. He doesn't want to get over his wife's passing. He wants to relive it every day because it's become his identity.

This is shadow at work.

This might sound uncommon, but I see many, many people who have found an identity in past pain that offers them an 'opt out' feature from life. One girl I knew was treated very badly by her first husband and it caused her to have a breakdown. But now, many years on, the abused wife is still her identity, and even though she has been offered many solid exit strategies from this identity she doesn't take them because it's too tasty where she is. Her anger is like a great big steak that she sinks her teeth into every single day. When I tried to offer a therapeutic outlet from her pain, she snarled at me, 'You don't know what he did to me.' I said, 'I don't need to know what he did to you. It doesn't matter what he did to you.' What does matter is that she heals from her past. But the shadow of anger is so strong that when you talk to her, you don't reach the real her, you are just talking to the shadow.

When my brother became an alcoholic we all despaired and ran around like headless chickens trying to stop him from drinking himself into an early grave. It became very clear to us after a while that we were no longer talking to my brother, we were talking to the bottle, and the bottle had become his shadow. I eventually got to see that very strong shadow leave my brother when he collapsed across a hospital bed with all his organs failing. My brother and some of my other alcoholic friends became so identified with their shadow that they defended it (or the shadow talking though them defended itself) to the death of their mortal coil. One friend lost a kidney because of drink, and even when the doctor told him that the drink was killing him, he was still in denial, defending his right to kill himself, saying, 'I've earned a drink. I've worked all my life for a beer.' He too lost his life before he lost his addiction.

Letting go

So my point is this: you are who you are, you are where you are and you are what you are. You are a product of every experience you have ever had and for some of us (well, for most of us) those experiences have left scars. In psychology these are called 'schemas' and each schema can be seen as one of the many hats that fear or shadow wears, because they all share the same base material: energy. In this case, specifically, energy that is trapped. In this text we are calling them shadows. They can be the bearer of great pain, but they can also be the harbinger of success and the cause of great celebration. Your pain is a potential treasure chest, and it is all yours. What I've learned about shadows and what I know is this: locked away inside you they are not healthy; they block the flow of natural energy in and through the body. I also know that most shadows are looking for an exit from the body, as though they're aware that they are somehow lost in a fleshy maze and are desperately looking to find a way out. Most of them do want to come out, they really do. You just need to help them find a way. But while the surface shadows will pop out easily enough, like peas from their pod, the more established shadows will not leave without a fight. They are like institutionalised prisoners who feel safer in their jail than they do on the outside. These are the little beggars that we have to trick out, starve out, shine out, lure out, coerce out, love out or even scare out. But they need to be out. Sometimes they will be jarred out by life situations like the death of a loved one, loss of a job, marriage breakdown or any number of other traumatic events, and when the shadow is jarred out it is a good opportunity to keep it out. Other times, when the shadows are ready to leave, the smallest most innocuous situations can act as a catalyst for release.

Let me tell you about one such situation from my own personal life. It involved a very deeply embedded shadow that I had to let go of, one that had been in me probably from the age of about eleven. It was at a time in my life when I was so ill that I thought I must be dying. Honestly. I exaggerate not. To the outside world I looked fine. I am a stoic so I didn't stop working; I didn't stop taking calls. I put my best face on and I fronted the world bravely. But, inside, something was passing over. It was a very ancient shadow. Inside it was kicking off like a crammed nightclub on a balmy night. Mentally I was crawling on all fours, moving very little, and praying much. I could tell you that it was dissolving because my beautiful dad was dying of cancer at the time and that the loneliness and fear and pain I saw playing out in his eyes had jarred my shadow free and had subsequently tipped me – and it did pain me – but it wasn't that. Well, let's just say that it wasn't only that.

I could also tell you that I was wobbled by two years of polishing a very personal stage play extolling my violent past, a savage catharsis that allowed me to exhume some ugly archetypes, place them on a stage and invite audiences to judge me. Or that the fifteen-year journey of structuring a screenplay about my struggles through depression, turned into a major and painful atonement. Or even that forty-seven years of personal purification, evicting shadows that fought a pitched and bloody battle to keep their residency, was finally taking its toll… But I won't because, while it did wobble me to invest so much of myself into projects that I struggled to bring to fruition, it was not ultimately this that threw me over the edge. Well, let's just say that it wasn't only this. My body looked all right to the world at large, but let me tell you that it didn't feel so splendid living inside an imploding mass of fleshy spaceship. My mind was impaired from multifarious struggles, and my internals churned like an industrial mincer. My bladder felt ravaged from an overworked and oversensitive Sympathetic Nervous System (either I couldn't piss, or I couldn't stop pissing, and there was not an hour or a minute of the day when I didn't feel the urge to piss, even on my long-distance runs, even in my sleep, even when there was not a fluid ounce left inside of me to vacate). I was sent to the hospital and tested for everything: prodded, poked, scrutinised and fingered. Sometimes by male doctors who searched for cancers in my most personal cavities, but who never once engaged my mental anguish, or by female doctors who had more empathy for the chair I sat in than they did for me, and occasionally, very occasionally I was embraced by wonderful human beings who permeated me with love and concern.

Some suggested that my pain was a symptom of trying to die for my dad (he had prostate cancer). And man, I did feel like dying for my dad, even though I innately knew that a thousand sacrificial deaths would not spare him even one night of torment. Others said I was a burnout, the victim of too much ambition and more work than a body could tolerate. More still suggested that I over-thought, over-sympathised and over-fucking-indulged my empathy for the pain of the world.

All of which is true. But none of these plunged me through all nine circles of the abyss. All of these things played minor parts in my demise, but none the lead role.

I knew what was wrong with me, and it would not be discovered in a blood test or an internal examination of my flesh.

The reason I was dying, the cause of my implosion, the root of my psychosomatic ills (that had manifested as physical agony) came down to one thing: I was scared, terrified actually, of losing my wife!

I was not scared of losing in a fight. And body parts were not on the list of things I feared losing either. A ravaged ear, a broken nose, distorted fingers pointing hideously in the wrong direction – merely badges of the battle I'd waged with life and I was perversely proud of them. In my Neanderthalic period I had been in many dozens of microcosmic wars on sticky nightclub carpets and on neon-lit pavements outside late-night chip shops, and with some killers too. Tooth and nail I fought, my lacerated and bulbous knuckles a record of every match, my scar-face a testimony to every caught blow.

No, I did not fear losing in a fight.

I was not afraid (interestingly enough) of losing my good health, only inasmuch as it might contribute to me losing my good wife. What young, desirable woman would want to carry an ailing male not capable of fighting, fucking or feeding the family (and all those other jobs that men think that women think are important)?

I was not afraid of illness, not even terminal. Cancer and its cohorts could go and fuck itself for all I cared. Death held no fear for me either. Honestly. Only... if I had cancer and had to spend some time in hospital, where a man cannot perform his role and function as a winner of bread, surely my wife would betray me, abandon me, leave me for some healthy virile with a backbone, someone... what's the word? Worthy. Someone worthy! And if I was dead... man, there is no way I could be dead; that would entail separation from my wife and that was a fear too big to even contemplate.

Cancer was only feared because it created a temporary separation (and vulnerability) and death only had one sting for me: losing Sharon.

This is what tipped me. And funnily enough this just-below-the-surface fear was jarred out of me by the most ridiculous of life situations. Sharon wanted to join a running club on her own. I was not invited. I know, I told you: ridiculous. But to me it felt like the four horsemen of the apocalypse had arrived on my doorstep and wanted to fight me one at a time on the front lawn.

As I said, internal shadows are always looking for an exit from the body, and those that do not volunteer are eventually forced out. And this was one that definitely needed a shove. I can only imagine that all of the previous shadows that I'd trained out, scared out or written out were layered on top this abandonment shadow and that their shift from my body left this one like a loose and throbbing tooth waiting to be pulled. Sharon joining the running club and leaving me at home proved to be the nudge that ripped it clean out.

However, this was not really about losing Sharon. This was not about being betrayed by Sharon, or abandoned. She was merely the focus of my fear, an old shadow finding shape, and if I had been married to Mother Teresa herself the fear would have been no less potent, because the fear was in the world of me, not in the world of men. Sharon and I were as tight as a folk singer's fringe. We were together all the time and there was no hint or premonition or threat of separation. Consciously I felt ridiculous; I was a grown man, I had four grown children and Sharon and I had been together (at the time) since the Dead Sea was still only ill. I also felt selfish and narcissistic. Or should I say a part of me felt selfish and narcissistic. My fear may seem silly, even ludicrous looking from the outside in, but to me it was as terrifying as climbing out of a dugout with a rifle, bayonet fixed and rushing into the no-man's-land of mortal combat. I realised that this fear had been in me for as long as I could remember, certainly it was there before me and Sharon, but because it had been left untreated it had grown and was now bursting out of my skin.

At the point of toppling I felt as though I was dying. My body certainly reacted as though I was dying. And I knew without hesitation that if I didn't deal with this growing demon soon, it was surely going to deal with me.

I was suffering from what psychologists call an 'abandon-ment schema'. Even though and even when everything and everyone around me held a safe assurance that I would not be abandoned I always, always, always felt as though I would. A needy, raw, savagely insecure part of me actually knew I would. To overcome this fear, to dissolve it, I had to let go of that part. The frightened child inside me that had been sexually assaulted and emotionally abandoned was the cause of all my pain, and he was also the key to all the freedom I could ever wish for. And no matter how many times people assured me and reassured me that I was safe and that I would not be abandoned, and that actually there is no such thing as abandonment, my fear still grew until my skin was too tight for it and was in danger of rupturing.

The solution was to let go. Let go.

Let go of the need for assurance and reassurance.

Let go of the false belief that I could be abandoned.

Let go of the childish need for certainty.

Let go of the false belief that I would not cope without my wife.

Let go of the need for clarity.

Let go of the false belief that I was not worthy.

Let go of Sharon!

Excuse me!!!! Are you fucking insane? What are you saying? Let go of Sharon…

You can fuck right off.

Let go. Let go of Sharon.

Even the words voiced in the safety of my own head were an abomination.

Fuck off!

Let her go.

Didn't you hear what I said, did you not hear the word I used (and not lightly, let me tell you)? *I am __terrified__!* (Underlined, bold and in italics, if you don't mind.)

And I might add, massively ashamed of my terror.

I have always been a warrior (I told myself unconvincingly). I thrive on uncertainty.

So why can't I let go?

At the time I was not even capable of saying the words out loud. I kid you not. It took me weeks and weeks of knee-wobbling anticipation before I could voice the words, and even then, when I did, it was spoken quickly and the words were sodden in sulk, like a teenager forced to make an apology in front of a parent.

I let go of Sharon.

The turning point came because of two things: 1) My fear had become so potent that my body could no longer contain it at the same time as staying healthy; and 2) I am a warrior. That is what I am. It is how I live. It is how I have always been. At school I faced down my bullies in the yard and on the fields after class, and as a young adult I chased away depression by becoming a hunter of shadows. I have always prided myself on the fact that I will not be bullied, not by people, not by out-of-control emotions and definitely not by irrational and untrue shadows.

There can be no bigger illusion than fear.

So I let go of Sharon. I dropped her like a brick that was very hot.

And here lies the revelation: in letting go of Sharon – who I feared losing more than my own life – I also (automatically) let go of the need to own, direct and control everything else inside and outside of my life.

Everything!

And I realised that in letting go I became free. And I became happy and so fucking light I nearly floated. And I discovered something wonderful: the things we cling onto control us, they actually imprison us. And when we let go we get to control the whole world.

When I was going through this scalding experience I just kept saying to myself (especially when the letting go was killing me), 'This is good. This is great. Actually, this is fucking fantastic!'

And it was fantastic, it is fantastic, and in the future, when I have to let go of more fears and the experience is a painful purification, it will be fantastic again.

In postscript I have to tell you that the letting go of this shadow was gradual, and to a degree it is still happening, but the results were and are profound. And as irony would have it, the more I let go of my wife, the closer we became. And I have never been so in love in my life.

As I said at the beginning of this chapter and I reiterate now, fear or shadow wears many hats but it has only one identity. It is energy and it's inside you, it is moving around and it wants to voice itself; in fact there are many shadows (many hats) inside of us queuing up waiting to have their say and find their exit. And if you don't actively help them find an exit they will eventually orchestrate situations in your life that force you to. Shadow is just trapped energy looking for an exit from the labyrinth that is your body. It wants to find its way out for all the right reasons; it is unhealthy to harbour trapped emotions, and if you are astute and look at these feelings sooner rather than later it does not have to be painful. It only tends to be painful because we resist it and when the shadow finally does start to leave we tense up and we fight it. Worst of all, we hide from it, like kids scared of the dark. And in hiding we expand our fear and make the situation worse. That's why hunting shadow is far less painful than being hunted by shadow; we are initiating the release of our own shadow rather than waiting for the process to be forced upon us. And let's be clear of one thing: eventually these shadows will out; it is going to happen, so you might as well be on the front foot and be a part of that transition. And you don't have to go inside and root around to find shadows, just move forward, out of any comfort zone and your shadows will emerge and show themselves. They will try and stop you, and in trying to stop you they will reveal their identity. And when they do they are already in the light and the transition has begun.

One of my great friends, Tony, has just found himself in such a situation. A normal working-class kid, he was doing well for himself; he'd become an international businessman and shared space with some of the most prolific business folk in the world. And the promotions were coming as thick as they were coming fast. In order to get to this position in his life he'd had to shed many old shadows. He was ascending high but starting to struggle because a deep-seated shadow, one that was formed when he was nearly murdered in a knife attack as a twelve-year-old, was holding him back. Like a man in a hot-air balloon he could not go any higher until he ditched the final sandbag that was weighing him down. It was after his last promotion, when he was asked to take over the position of international manager, that he tipped. Something inside him, his old shadow, did not want the responsibility of this top job, so gave him a dousing of fear to hold him back. But Tony is a hardy fellow. He didn't get to where he was in life without negotiating a little fear. So he pushed on, despite the fact that he was waking up early every morning dripping with sweat and feeling terrified of the day ahead. His shadow was doing everything to stop him from taking on this new position, and when it became clear that Tony was not going to back down, the shadow, that depressed part of him locked inside for the past twenty-five years, decided to abandon ship. It was a shadow that didn't want to leave, but when placed in a position that it felt it could no longer tender it decided it had to. And this is when the depression came for Tony. Depression is just an old depressed part of you that is leaving, and as it exits, certainly temporarily, that depression can become you. I have to say here that Tony didn't actually know what was going on inside his body, he didn't know about shadows or trapped emotions looking for an exit, or vices demanding a voice, certainly not on a conscious level. All he knew was that he felt terrible and sad and depressed. It was only when he went to see a wonderful therapist (Claire Boot, www.emotivecoaching.com) and sat down to talk that he realised he'd been holding this shit in, feeding it and inadvertently protecting it for as long as he could remember. When he sat with the therapist she helped the shadow out. It turned out that when Tony had been stabbed as a young lad, his friend was also been stabbed at the same time and had died on the pavement in front of him. The lad who stabbed them both was a cousin of Tony's. Because he was a relative the situation created mayhem in the family, resulting in Tony feeling (and at times actually being) abandoned by the people closest to him. When he was in hospital no one visited him. Not even his parents. In a bid to try and separate themselves from this hideous debacle they pulled away and tried to pretend that nothing had happened. This left young Tony with the physical scars of the stabbing and the deeper psychological and emotional scars of being betrayed and abandoned by his family. He'd tried to talk to them about it many times, but to no avail. They were not interested; in fact, they were in complete denial. After his breakdown he tried again. This time his family called him all sorts of unsavoury names for dragging up things that they didn't want to look at. Tony had to come to terms with and accept the fact that, even though he could see that many of his siblings were going through a similar trauma to him because of this collective shadow, it was their choice and their right not to look at it if they didn't want to. But Tony had no choice; he had to look at it. His sanity demanded no less. At the age of thirty-eight this shadow finally found its way out and, although he went through a difficult ordeal, he is now free from it. Because he's lighter, he's been able to make the transition at work and his life has never been better.

It is all just energy. It is trapped. It wants to come out. Help it to come out. Find an outlet and make the experience liberating and profitable, otherwise you'll end up looking and feeling like a Muñoz sculpture, blocked and immobile and ready to burst.

Chapter 5

The Muñoz Ball

I have to tell you the story of how I found the Muñoz ball (then I will tell you what the Muñoz ball is). I was in London for a few meetings to do with my work in film, so I thought it might be a good idea to try and catch up on a bit of art while I was in the capital. I'm always looking for inspiration and there can be few better places to find it than in a gallery or a museum. Art is on the bleeding edge when it comes to innovation, and artists are those very brave souls who place their wild imaginings into oils, watercolours and sculpture. Even if I don't always get the art itself I do love it and I am inspired by the courage it takes to be the very first to create something. Anyway, as I said, I am always looking for inspiration to fuel me and to fire my own imagination (and to clear shadow), so while I was in the city I thought I might spend a little time at the Tate Modern. There was a new exhibition on and I decided to go along. As is often the case when you're being guided by the Invisible Hand, I went along to one exhibition only to be hijacked by another. I'd already bought my ticket to get into the exhibition and decided with my wife Sharon to have a quick cup of tea before we went in, so we walked towards the canteen. As we entered, foraging for some tea and biscuits, I was stopped in my tracks. I saw two angels. Honestly. I was stunned. High on the wall was a life-sized sculpture of two completely whitewashed men sat on a park bench talking. But it was not the sculpture of the men that took my eye; it was the fact that the ceiling and wall lights had cast a shadow behind the sculpture giving the impression that both men had large and very distinctive wings: angel wings. I exclaimed excitedly to my wife, 'Angels!' like a ten-year-old who had just spied Father Christmas at the grotto. My wife gave me one of those looks (she is used to my antics) and said, 'What?' I pointed to the sculpture excitedly, my mind already racing: the shadow, the wings, the angels! She followed my finger and her eyes landed on… a sculpture of two men on the wall talking on a park bench.

'Angels!'

There, I'd said it again, the second time. My wife looked at me, frowning and puzzled. 'Wings,' I said. She looked again and saw nothing angelic, just the sculpture and a vague shadow. 'That,' I said with great emphasis, 'is an angel. Well, two angels.' She disagreed, so I approached one of the gallery assistants to prove my point. I pointed out the sculpture and I told the assistant that I particularly loved the way the lights were set so that the shadow made the men appear to have wings, like angels. Another blank look, then an apology, then an explanation: she told me that they'd had problems with lighting this particular sculpture and that the shadows were not supposed to be there. She picked up a book from the table that had a photograph of the exact same sculpture on the front cover page and… it had no wings. I have to tell you that I was not embarrassed or surprised. The fact that she couldn't see the wings and the fact that Sharon couldn't see the wings, and as far as I could ascertain neither could anyone else in the canteen, told me that perhaps only I was supposed to see the angels. It was a sign. I like signs, I love serendipity, and I love the fact that when God wants you to see something He will send angels to point the way. I was already inspired, and I hadn't even been into the exhibition yet.

As it turned out the sculpture that I admired so much, my angel sculpture (and let us be in no doubt here, this was not fanciful imagination, they were definitely and unequivocally angels) was not even a part of the exhibition I was here to see; it was part of an entirely separate collection by a completely different sculptor, a Spanish artist (now sadly deceased) called Juan Muñoz. I knew that I had to go and see this exhibition, and immediately. So I bought my tickets and in I went. Several rooms were filled with the most splendid and the most unusual sculptures, but there were two particular designs that spoke to me and that gave me the inspiration for this chapter. The first was called *Last Conversation Piece* (see illustration).

Last Conversation Piece consists of sculptures of people, sometimes in large groups standing around, and other times just single figures standing alone. The representations are grotesque distortions of normal men and women, emerging out of very large balls. You can't see their legs; it is as though the ball represents their whole lower half, from feet to torso. The figures have no open orifices. The mouth, eyes and ears are all blocked, and because of the huge ball at their base and the lack of discernable legs the figures are completely immobile. I got the feeling that these figures couldn't see, hear, speak or move (I have to state here that this is just my impression and not necessarily what Juan Muñoz intended). They all have strikingly similar features, perhaps representing the sheep-mentality, where almost everyone is the same; there are no individuals. The sculpture represented to me the imprisoned man, locked immobile by his own unutilised energy. The blocked orifices spoke to me of men and women who have no receptive inlet for light and no oral, visual or tactile outlet for creativity. The huge ball at their base represented to me a logjam, the blocked and backlogged creative energy, the trapped and imprisoned shadow. And the immobility was every man and every woman who ever had a dream but was wheel-locked by the weight of their own fears. When I looked at *Last Conversation Piece*, I was looking at the young me, a beautiful boy who was terribly blocked and imprisoned by his own shadows.

I realised immediately that in order for the blocked man to become free of the Muñoz ball and thus mobile and creative again, he has to engineer his own outlets for the shadow; he has to manually open his eyes to the world (people are often deliberately blind to their potential because they fear their potential, and blind to their own shadows for the same reason), open his mouth to articulate his shadow free and open his ears so that he can hear the truth, because the truth will always set you free.

Fear or shadow energy that is not used for physical creation stultifies us; it creates physical, psychological, physiological and spiritual constipation. Blake says it beautifully in his poem 'Proverbs of Hell': 'he who desires but acts not, breeds pestilence'. And that pestilence is the subsequent Muñoz ball, a huge mass of blocked energy that keeps us rooted in small realities. Understanding the Muñoz ball enables us to create visual, auditory, verbal, written and tactile outlets for the creative use of our shadow.

Towards the Shadow

The other sculpture that I found fascinating was not immediately apparent to me on the day of the exhibition; it came to me much later, during the writing of this book. When I went back into Muñoz to revisit *Last Conversation Piece*, I found a second sculpture that had a profound effect on me, not least because it mirrored so closely the words that I'm presently writing about hunting the shadow. Eerily, the sculpture is called *Towards the Shadow* (see illustration).

It is a piece that Juan Muñoz created to touch upon the themes of violence and disaster, something that he did throughout all of his work. *Towards the Shadow* suggests the aftermath of a crash. It is the magnification of a street scene in which a car is glimpsed on a large screen heading towards the sculpture of a man whose arms are spread from his sides, as though in fearful anticipation of the impending collision. The light from the car headlamps hits the man first, casting his shadow large on the wall behind him. Muñoz saw this as a representation of the man's monstrous alter ego (his shadow). What this underlined to me is that shadow needs a healthy outlet from the body and if we don't give it one it will create a crash in our lives (in this case the crash is literal, with a car) to force it out. My crash as a young man was a debilitating depression; my friend Tony's crash was a breakdown; for others that crash might be marriage problems, redundancy, illness, etc. Any challenging life situation can act as the crash that jars our shadow free, and ultimately liberates us from it.

But here's the point: I don't think we need to wait for crashes and devastation and breakdowns to free our shadow. I think this is just shadow working on its own because we won't work with it. I believe that if we are pre-emptive with our shadows, if we are perceptive and brave and we go out into the night, as Rumi suggested, and hunt down our fears, the shadows will pop out with the littlest of effort and smallest of discomforts.

Everyone is individual, of course, and we all have to find our own way of freeing ourselves by freeing our shadow. I think it's best to do this as a two-pronged assault: find as many ways as possible (as many inlets as possible) to fill yourself with light, thus dissolving any darkness that is left inside you, also finding as many outlets as is humanly possible to give a creative exit for your shadow.

Investing in yourself

For me the inlets are what I eat and drink and ingest in the form of foodstuffs (we talked about the importance of this earlier). They are also what I hear, what I see and what I touch. I make sure that my impressions and conversations (with others and with myself) are empowering, enlightening and inspiring. I listen only to very inspirational radio, music, theatre and talks (tape or Internet) by empowering and congruent people. What you read is also, of course, what you hear, because you sub-vocalise the written word in your own head. So spend money and invest in the very best that the high street bookshops or Amazon have to offer. Try and invest a great proportion of your earned wealth back into the very profitable business that is you. Huge companies like Red Bull reinvest up to a third of their revenue back into their own company so that they can grow their core business. How much do you reinvest? And if you are not reinvesting in you, why not? If you don't invest in yourself, who else will? I spend thousands of pounds every year on books, films, audio and life experience so that I can educate, stimulate and inspire myself.

The power of music

Music has a profound effect on the human body, and great music can play a powerful role in dissolving shadow, because it brings light into the body and it jars or shifts shadow. In the ancient Chinese oracle, the I Ching, it says that music is a direct link to God, and theatre, film, art and so on are an extension of music, so listening to music or looking at art can be a great inlet for light. Just avoid the soap and the porn that many programmes proffer.

I was recently in Paris, France promoting a film we've just shot, and I made a point when I was there of going to see (and touch) the iconic places, like the Eiffel Tower, The Arc de Triomphe and so on. I also took a day out to visit one of my favourite sculptors, Rodin, at The Rodin Museum. It's one thing to view these magnificent sculptures (*The Thinker, The Infernal Tunnel, The Gates of Hell*) from the pages of a book, but it is an entirely different experience when you see them in real life and you touch the sculpture that the artist himself worked on. You actually get to touch a part of him, because he has placed himself into his work. And it's not an ephemeral experience that disappears when you climb on the metro and go back to your hotel. These kinds of experience are often so profound that they stay with you (and they give you light) forever. What was once a part of Rodin actually becomes a part of you. And any time you want to, you can recall the experience and feel that light all over again. I have a friend, Warner – an entrepreneur – who, along with his lovely wife Karan, pretty much travels the globe just so that he can experience the art and the culture of great men and women past and present (at the writing of this book he is exploring Dubai with a wonderful poet friend of ours called Wael – www.waelalsayegh.com) and his search is having a profound and moving effect not just on him and his life, but on everyone around him. Similarly, the Paris experience was one of the very best of my life, not least because my gorgeous wife Sharon and I walked all the way back from The Rodin Museum to our hotel, which took us about an hour and a half. We strolled hand in hand all the way along the River Seine. We passed just about every great view that Paris has to offer.

Similarly, a few years ago I spent a memorable few days in London stopping at the wonderful Groucho Club, and concluded my stay with a trip to the theatre to watch Patrick Stewart in his one-man version of the famous Dickens story *A Christmas Carol* in the West End. It was not only mesmerising, it was inspirational. For days afterwards we talked about how amazing it was, and my mind raced with exciting ideas about the things I could perhaps write for a London theatre and how I might be able to pen words that are beautiful enough for Patrick Stewart to act. This one visit to the theatre (and it would have been easy not to have gone; there is the cost, the organisation, the bother – inspiring and investing in yourself takes courage and it takes effort) had a transformational effect upon me. Not only did it act as an inlet for inspiration, vital in dissolving shadows, but it also inspired me to want to put on a successful West End play, the writing of which would, in the future, unseat other old and established shadows.

Don't forget that the older the shadow, the more likely it is to want to stay put. It will not take kindly to you leaving the comfort zone to have exotic and (to its mind) dangerous experiences, things that are going to make it vulnerable.

So fill your life with art, fill your office or your house (and your head) with culture, make sure that every inlet is open to light, and then place yourself before the glare.

The sense of touch is also a great way of inletting love and light. Even the perceived sense of touch (imagining being touched) can have a profound effect on the human psyche. When I was going through a particularly difficult purification period I would sit myself down, close my eyes and imagine very vividly walking through a country park with my wife Sharon. I'd imagine her hand in mine, her warm fingers caressing me, I imagined her kissing me and the smile she makes that says 'I am in love'. I could get the feeling so intense that my whole body would lighten up and tingle and the dark feelings that were inside me were swamped and dissolved.

When Victor Frankle was going through hell in the concentration camps of World War Two and it looked as though he might not last another day, he would access his estranged wife in his imagination and have the most profound and enlightening conversations with her as they walked hand in hand back in their home village. He recalls in his wonderful book *Man's Search for Meaning* that his visions were so vivid it felt as real as if she was actually standing there with him.

I am a tactile person, so I pass on my love to people very much through my hands; I touch people quite a lot as I speak. Words are also tools for passing on love and for receiving love from others. But I feel it mostly through touch. And of course I like being touched too; this is probably why I enjoyed wrestling so much, because you get to physically connect with people in the most profoundly personal way, even if you might not know them that well (it is common in judo and wrestling to visit different clubs and wrestle with complete strangers). Don't be afraid to touch (especially you men out there) and don't be afraid of being touched either, or even of asking to be touched. It is a great inlet for love and light and a vital tool in shadow hunting.

There are many possible outlets for your shadow, but I find that the creative outlet works best. I don't know why this is, but shadow seems to be more amenable to a creative outlet, perhaps because the energy you are releasing will find a new and a useful life in art. I know for me, personally, that the great majority of my shadow has been (and still is) exorcised and transmuted into words on the page, words that actually go on to serve others. I have written books, articles, plays, films, sketches and even letters, and the very best stuff has all been transmuted shadow, drawn right from the coal face. I know of other people, Jimmy Boyle for instance (his story can be seen in the great film *Sense of Freedom*), who turned their shadow into sculpture. Many Auschwitz survivors found great catharsis in writing music, creating art, writing books about their experiences, touring the world and giving inspirational talks. Similarly, victims of childhood abuse often find an outlet in art; there is even art therapy available now, and drama therapy. Some people create in the garden and spend their shadows in nature. My lovely friend Mark Wood might be a shit bricklayer, but he is a wonderful Christian healer (www.outpouringheart.co.uk), and he finds his absolution in serving others. Because of this he heals himself by healing them. Everyone is different, but I do guarantee you one thing: there will be a specific and unique way for you to outlet your trapped emotions. You just have to find it.

Letters from America

When my daughter Lisa was living in America away from all her family and friends and struggling with personal fears, she found solace in prayer and prolific letter writing. They acted as great balm to her. Interestingly, once she was back home and no longer sad, she found that her letter writing dried up, as though her shadow had been completely removed and made beautiful in rafts of correspondence that she sent across the ocean to me and the other people in her life that she loved (but me especially, I think). I have seen manically depressed people cure themselves through running. I have witnessed people mourning the death of a loved one healed simply by spending their energy in a gym. Another friend was diagnosed by his doctor as a paranoid schizophrenic; he joined our wrestling group and used the training and influences as a kind of hybrid physical therapy and was able eventually to come off medication, cure himself and live not only a normal life, but a great life.

Nothing is impossible; you just need to open the inlet and fill yourself with light, and find the right outlets for all the shadow that is inside you so that you dissolve your pestilence and spend all that energy blocked in your Muñoz ball.

But before you can do that you need one very vital ingredient. You need purpose.

Chapter 6

Purpose

This chapter is about recognising the need for and understanding the power of purpose. It is about finding purpose if your life lacks it, enhancing purpose if yours feels weak and staying in contact with your purpose throughout your life, because if you forget why you are on the path, you will certainly fall off the path.

This is the difficult chapter.

Finding a purpose that will inspire and encourage you to challenge your fears and clear your shadow would, you'd think, be easy enough, and yet some people are given what you might consider to be the ultimate purpose from their doctors when they are told 'stop smoking or you will die' and they still don't manage to stop smoking. Others are told that if they don't lose weight they will be dead in two years; they still don't lose weight. More still are warned that they will lose their children if they don't stop drinking to excess (this happened to a relative of mine); they still don't stop drinking. It would seem that even the threat of death and losing your children is not enough of a purpose for some people. And yet, you hear stories all the time about amazing transformations that occur for the oddest of reasons: the obese woman who sees her reflection in a shop window and is so horrified by how large she has become that she vows there and then to lose the weight, and she does; a lad on the way to alcoholism overhears someone talking about him, saying that his drinking is ruining his girlfriend's life, and he is so upset by the revelation that he never touches a drop again. Another man, a friend of mine called Bob Sykes, was stuck in the mill working a job that he hated but was terrified to leave. Suddenly he found his purpose after one of his workmates told him arrogantly, 'You'll be here for life, just like me.' He packed his job in the same afternoon, started teaching martial arts full time and went on to run an international martial arts magazine (www.martialartsltd.co.uk).

Everyone's purpose in life is so individual that it is difficult to predict what it might be through the pages of a book. I only know that purpose is a huge force and once you click into it, once it has been found there is nothing you will be unable to achieve. The pounds will drop off, the addictions will die and the marathon that you have always wanted to run will run itself. It is a given. All of the great discoveries and all of the amazing feats and the most beautiful art have always been powered by purpose. It is so commanding that it excites me even writing about it, because it reminds me that if I want to be a successful member of the human race and if I want to access true power and tread the world stage with my passion, all I need to do is find my purpose.

PURPOSE

When I look back on my life and I recall those very successful moments I can see that victory was always purpose-driven. And equally, if I recall the times that I failed to complete a project or when I didn't win or succeed, I can see with retrospect that they were the times when I didn't have sufficient purpose, and so I ran out of steam.

Purpose is always difficult to find, but it is so potent once discovered that it is well worth the search. It was purpose that got Victor Frankle safely through the concentration camps (after the war he even developed his own system to help people find their purpose called Logo Therapy: www.logotherapy.univie.ac.at). He said that his purpose (to survive and tell the world of the atrocities) was so strong that the whole universe conspired to keep him alive. On many occasions he avoided almost certain death because serendipity and universal happenstance redirected him at the very last second. It was purpose that took Lance Armstrong from a dying cancer patient to a healthy eight-time winner of the Tour de France (see his great book *It's Not About the Bike*). Armstrong became a furnace of activity and used everything and anything as fuel to heal himself, even devouring negative newspaper articles written about him, to use as a source of energy. His purpose was so powerful that nothing could get in his way.

So while I can't tell you here and now what your specific purpose is (only you know that), I can offer you a few ideas that might help trigger the sense of purpose in your mind. I like to think that purpose is a *happy accident*. I don't quite know how and why and when it will happen, but I do know how you can make yourself accident prone, and more likely to make this magic occur. Remember this: when you have a very strong desire for change, you will find your purpose.

You are your own alpha and your own omega

A few years ago I was overweight; I was nearly sixteen stone. I knew enough even then to know that when we overeat it's because we are not just feeding ourselves, we are also feeding our shadow. Any addictions that we have, and all of our excesses, are shadow feed. When we are looking for instant gratification, even though we know it's not healthy, it's not us being greedy and impatient, it is our shadow. And when we're tempted to take inappropriate (perhaps illegal) short-cuts at work or in life, even though it's highly irregular, this is not us either, it's our shadow. The guy that has illicit affairs and ruins marriage after marriage is feeding shadow. The gossip is feeding shadow. The judgemental? A gorging shadow. The dishonest and the violent, all of them are serving shadow. The man who takes drugs, drinks too much and overeats is feeding his shadow. Internet porn is an easy trap for shadow. Drink and drugs are like fertiliser for our trapped emotions. This is why it is so vital for you to kill your addictions and curb your excesses, because they are all keeping your shadow alive.

Back to me.

I was tall and I was muscular so most people would probably just have looked at me and thought, He's a big bloke. They would not have immediately seen me as a fat person, and because I was a martial artist and wrestler I could get away with a bit of extra timber. But I knew in myself, even if others didn't. I was a master grade in the martial arts but I knew deep down that I was no master. I couldn't even control basic diet so I could hardly claim to be a master. I really wanted to lose weight, and I really wanted to be what it said on the tin but I just couldn't find a strong enough purpose. The thought of being a self-sovereign, a captain of my own destiny, a modern-day shaman was what really intrigued me; I knew that if I could control the basics, get my food right, live a clean and honest life, eschew all my nasty habits (the ones that were feeding this shadow), I would be on my way. What really excited me though, what really gave me the initial spark of purpose, was the fact that I knew deep down in my heart that until I got a handle on these basics I was never going to gain access to the big spiritual stuff that I knew was out there waiting for me. No one in their right mind is going to put you on the mountain while you are still struggling with a hill. This is why I decided to search for a purpose: so that I could expand my conscious net and gain access to God. My search started in meditation. Every day I sat down, quieted my thoughts and visualised myself looking and feeling slim and in control. I went deeply into the visualisation, until I was actually, in my mind's eye, in the body and in the life that that I wanted to inhabit. Looking back I can see that it was my definite intent that started the universal orchestration. I absolutely and unequivocally did intend to become a master of myself (and slim to boot). That was the beginning. Then things started to feel different in my life: I felt the urge to train more, I felt the urge to eat less and make healthier food choices, and the thought of overeating or eating junk food started to feel repugnant. I began to eat lighter meals, and I started to eat more often (eating small and often speeds up the metabolic rate and helps you to lose weight), books came into my orbit (many of them sent through the post free from people who thought I might enjoy them) that inspired and informed me, I met people serendipitously who had vital information to help me on my quest. All of a sudden I was three stone lighter and feeling wonderful. And it is no coincidence that the moment my weight came down and I became more balanced, my writing got better, my business grew, my relationship with friends and family and loved ones thrived, I started to attract awards and contracts for my work and I accessed the most amazing ideas – sometimes they just popped into my head. Clearing these shadows allowed me to gradually see and attract and create more and more in my life. And this gave me the incentive to become more constant with my balance, more diligent with my eating and my daily habits, because the more I mastered myself the more the universe (God) brought my way. I was basically getting everything that I could handle, and this made me want to build the internal infrastructure (by clearing shadows) to be able to handle more. And this in itself became my purpose.

So my purpose started with a very strong and definite intent. Then I paid attention to my intent, I meditated on it, visualised clearly the end result, and this in turn started the universal orchestration that brought as much booty to my door as I could handle.

I watched the same thing happen with my son Louis. He was overweight, his clothes didn't fit properly which made him stressed, he stopped grooming himself because he felt fat in everything (so 'what's the point?') and this caused more stress, which made him grumpy, and when he was grumpy he'd gorge himself on fast food and sugary drinks. It became a vicious cycle and he was getting fatter and fatter; in the end he had to put his belt on with a lasso. He became so out of balance that he literally created a centrifugal force field that pushed everyone, including his family, away from him. At college everything had suddenly become hard work, the things he normally loved doing were all going wrong (and none of it was his fault) and even the inspirational music teacher he used to rave on about all the time had suddenly morphed into someone that 'just don't get it'. For a very long time I tried to speak with him about it, I tried to encourage him to change (he was getting unhealthily big and very negative) and I even left motivational books on his bed in a bid to try and inspire him into action, but none of it worked. Part of the problem was that most of his influences at that time, outside of the family unit, were fat, lazy people. They were all nice folk, I liked them a lot, but they were not dynamic in any sense. Louis borrowed their shadows and became the same as them. In the end, in a last ditch attempt at getting him to do something with himself, I sat and had a very hard and honest and painful chat with him. I told him how I felt, how worried I was about him, and how weak he had become, following easy influences and becoming a slave to his body and abandoning many of the dreams he'd been following since he was a boy. I told him that I loved his bones, but that I could no longer sit and listen to his whining and his excuse-making and that if he wanted to be fat and lazy, that was OK with me; it was his choice, as long as he didn't expect me to sit and listen to his negativity. The honesty was just my way of saying, 'I am worried that if you keep living this way I will lose you, because fat kids do not make their pension.'

He argued back, of course; he was defending his friends, he was defending his girl and he was defending his lifestyle but the shock of my words got through. Realising that his negative actions affected everyone else (in a bad way), not least the girlfriend with whom was in love, triggered Louis's purpose to be a master of himself, to be responsible with his life choices and to be his own gospel by living his life as healthily as possible.

Once he realised that he was the captain of his own destiny, that he was his own alpha and his own omega, he became inspired to do something about it. He made the changes, he lost the weight and I got my son back. And he became like a magnet; suddenly this balanced and beautiful young man was attracting job offers, beautiful girlfriends and free tuition from some of the best martial artists in the world. It was an amazing spectacle to see. It inspired me.

The search

Purpose is there. Let us be clear, there can be no doubt about that. You are sitting in and around your purpose as we speak; you just can't see it yet. And you can't see it because your shadow is hiding it. Why would it hide your purpose? Because purpose is the beginning of the end of shadow, that's why. But if you have an undeniable intent (which is different from a wish or a distant desire) your purpose will appear in front of you miraculously. So your first purpose is to find your purpose, and that on its own is a very powerful and potent force: the universe will hear your call and it will start to move in your favour. To find anything, you need to start with a search, and the moment you start your search all sorts of miraculous things that you would never have imagined will be orchestrated in your life to help you. The process really is magical. When I'm looking for a particular purpose, my happy accident, I always start with inspiration. Inspiration is light, and light dissolves shadow, and sitting behind shadow is your purpose. If I wanted to build an amazing physique I would read bodybuilding magazines and start visiting gyms and talking to weightlifters and generally surrounding myself with all things physique-related. I spoke earlier about inadvertently borrowing shadow from other people. Well, on the positive side, you can borrow light from other people too. If you are associated with positive people, that positive aura is infectious; like shadow it jumps from person to person, but unlike shadow light makes you want to be an amazing human being. Even if you just read about a positive person, someone who has achieved great things, the light will jump across. This is one of the reasons why books and magazines and articles about the inspiring and the successful are so popular. You can purchase a little light, simply by investing in a book. If you keep reading, surround yourself by fellow enthusiasts (in whatever endeavour you wish to master) and invest as much of your day as possible in the pursuit of your purpose you will fill yourself more and more with light, until eventually the shadow that is hiding your true purpose will be dissolved.

The shadow energy will keep moving around inside you trying to avoid the light, and it will keep throwing negativity at you in a bid to pull you from the path, but eventually you'll read one line in a book, or hear one conversation, or you will have a sudden realisation and *bang!* The shadow will be gone and your purpose will be as clear as the page in front of you. The moment that purpose is clear, you are in the most powerful position you will ever be in. And it can happen in the blink of an eye, but you must first build the momentum by gradually immersing yourself in your search.

Full commitment, full immersion

When I wanted to gain a black belt in judo, a very difficult task that few people achieve and one that takes a very strong purpose, I did exactly that. I gradually immersed myself in the world of judo. At first, I had interest and I had desire and I had intent but the purpose was not fully formed. So I read about judo, I watched DVDs of great judo players in action and I found an instructor who was prepared to teach me privately. I built myself up with twice-a-week private judo sessions, to see if this was where I really wanted to be and if there was enough in judo to take my desire to a fully formed purpose. I knew that I needed to learn judo because, at the time, I was a professional martial arts instructor and grappling was my weak range. But I knew that it was a very big commitment. I was forty years of age and not sure if perhaps I had left it a little late for such a physical art, so dipping my toe into the water and making a partial commitment was my way of seeing if there was enough there to get me fired up. There was. I loved it, every minute of it, and I was quite a natural so my progress was quick. I became very inspired then to get my black belt, so I started to up my commitment. My friend Neil Adams, former world judo champion and a double Olympic silver medallist, ran a full-time class for international players. He invited me to join them. Another big commitment, not just because it was extra training but because I was training with members of the Olympic squad. My wife was actually worried that I might get dropped on my head and break my neck – a very real concern when you are fighting with some of the best players in the world. Luckily these were nice, gentle folk and they took it easy on me until I found my feet. I committed myself to one session a week with Neil. Just one. I could handle one session a week. One session quickly became two, and two three, and before very long I was training every day. In fact, I was training full-time hours, with Neil and with my other training friends. I found my purpose. And interestingly I can't actually tell you specifically what that purpose was (sometimes it is very hard to put purpose into words – my wife loves to run for instance, but she does not know exactly why, only that she loves to run), only that I knew with every fibre of my being that I needed to be on the judo mat every day. I wanted it like a drowning man wants air. So, I completely immersed myself in reading, writing about, watching and practising judo every day. All of my friends were judo players on the world stage. Judo became my whole life for two years. I got my black belt, and not just that; I became a seasoned judoka who did not look out of place in an international class.

My purpose was found because I searched diligently like a man hunting for treasure. Every stage of the way required more commitment, a little bit more effort and time; every new level demanded more of me than I thought I could give and at every new stage a voice in my head asked, 'How much do you want this?' until in the end it asked everything of me and I happily gave it all, because I loved every minute of what I was doing. Not that it wasn't hard – at times it was bone-achingly difficult – and not that I didn't have moments of serious doubt. Both of my ears were cauliflowered in practice and many times I lay my beaten body in a hot bath after training and thought, I don't know if I can go on. But I did and the rewards were worth it. Practising judo at this level didn't just gain me a black belt; it gave me a character that could not have been forged in any other arena. It transformed who I am.

And this has been true for me in every endeavour I have undertaken, from martial arts, to risking my life as a nightclub doorman (now there is a commitment!), right through to this day working my way up the echelons as a screenwriter where every script demands a part of my soul and every single rebuttal (and there have been many) makes me feel like selling up, living in a tent by the sea and sacking the whole damn lot. Success in life asks everything of you – that is one thing I am sure of. And if you are trying to be the best at something and you are not prepared to give it your all then you are already walking backwards (even if you think you are moving ahead) down the wrong path. One of the main reasons people don't find their gold is because they don't want it enough. They don't have the purpose, and if they don't have the purpose it's because they're not hungry enough to make finding their purpose their first purpose. But let me be clear about what I am not saying: I am not saying that you have to sacrifice your wife or neglect your children or risk your good health for success. Not at all. When I talk about giving it everything you have, I mean giving it your full attention, giving it your full commitment, investing yourself completely in the process. You can do this and still have a life, you can still have a great relationship with your kids and you can still give yourself to your partner. They can all come along for the ride.

I have a friend who is massively successful in the City. He is a wonderful man. When he first went into trading he decided that he was going to become the best, but he was only going to work from eight to five, and at night and at the weekend he was going to switch his phone off and dedicate himself to his family. He was told by his friends and his colleagues that he would not make it. 'It's not possible!' they said. But he did make it, and he made it big because he decided that this was what he was going to do. And he is a true success because he didn't wreck his health and lose his family – he had it all. He did fewer hours that his friends and work colleagues, but because he had less time to work with he made every second count.

The Jeep Syndrome

By aiming high and by deliberately restricting the time he had to achieve his goal he accidentally triggered what I call 'The Jeep Syndrome'. During World War One, the US Army needed a fast, lightweight, all-terrain vehicle. And they needed it urgently. Normally it can take years to design and make a vehicle, but because of the nature of the situation this amount of time was not available to them. In 1940, the Army called on the automotive companies to create a working prototype (fitting army specifications) within forty-nine days. Willy's Truck Company was the first to create the right prototype. The new vehicle was nicknamed 'the Jeep'. General Dwight D. Eisenhower said that America could not have won World War Two without it.

Forty-nine days! Can you imagine that? Well, Willy's Truck Company could and they did, and they got the contract and the Jeep is still being used by armies (and in civi-street) all over the world today. What my city friend did was accidentally fall into this syndrome by only allowing himself a limited timeframe in which to become the best. Success is not success if you make yourself ill and you lose your family in the process.

I intend to be massively successful, and that means having it all. And as long as you make that your definite purpose, you will have it all, so start searching now. Not later today, not tomorrow, not next week or after you come back from your holiday. Now. Don't put this off, because if you do you'll stall, and then you have to start all over again. Pick up a book, get onto the Internet, ring a friend, start collecting the inspiration you need to clear your shadow, make it your full-time job to find purpose and watch the magic start to happen. You will be amazed at the amount of help you will get if you only start. There is a very wise and true old saying: 'If you turn towards God, God will run towards you.' In other words, all you have to do is turn in the right direction and all the help you could possibly want will come your way. And if you turn away again, all that help will disappear. It's you who starts the magic, and it's you who stops it. You are the magic! Of this I am very sure. You have to initiate it; if you wait for the inspiration it will not come and the muse is legendary for abandoning folk who are short on intention and big on blame. There is no one to blame; you are your only friend and you are your only enemy. The moment you initiate the search the whole of the cosmos will become your ally, and the moment you start to look for people to blame even the constellations will conspire against you. That is because the On/Off switch is in you. You are the creator, and you create with every thought you have, with every word you utter and with every deed you do. The universe does not work in right and wrong, good and bad, favourable and unfavourable. It just creates your every intention. That is the universal law; what you pay attention to will grow and what you take attention away from will atrophy. So what you deem as good or bad is merely a human judgement, as far as the universe is concerned. It just provides the thing you place your consistent, emotive attention on. It delivers your order, and even though you might think you don't want it, you did order it. Most people spend their days thinking and talking about what they don't want and then look surprised when it keeps turning up. They are amazed when they can't get through the door because their horns are too big. That's where their attention is, so that's what they create. If you don't want something in your life, stop thinking about it, stop investing your emotive energy into it, and kill all of the influences around you that are adding their attention to your attention and helping you to build a world full of wrong things.

Do not underestimate shadow

Once you begin you have to keep the momentum going. Many people start this journey only to be drawn from the path after a few hours or a few days or even a few years. When you start clearing shadows, they are often strong and you have a real fight on your hands, but once you clear them they lose all their power to influence you. But know this: shadows are tricky customers and will always be waiting on the periphery for a vulnerability that will allow them back in again. Do not underestimate your shadow. My friend packed in smoking for five years, and he really felt that he'd whipped his addiction. Then a work colleague died and my mate went to his funeral. He met a few old mates there, one of them said to him, 'This is so upsetting. I'm going to have a cigarette.' And then he offered one to my friend and... well, I guess you know the rest. It's a common story. Ten years later and he's still addicted and his chest is wheezing like an old accordion.

The shadow will use any situation and enlist the help of other shadows to get you off the right path, it will orchestrate events in your life to put you off, entice you off, seduce you and even scare you off the path. Be prepared; the shadow can be very ingenuous. It is very good at taking you away from the scent and even convincing you that not only is it a good idea to abandon all hope, but it's *your* idea to abandon all hope.

I had another friend who found her purpose to stop feeding her shadow and lose weight. She lost three stone in a short time and she was a new woman. She got rid of all the junk food from her life and she was training and eating very healthily. Her high blood pressure dropped to a normal level, she had energy and as her waistline shrunk her business expanded. I had never seen her so happy. Then she had a visit from an old friend, someone from her past that she used to enjoy socialising with. Part of their social ritual was to share wine and a pizza and a tub of ice cream. My friend rang me the next day and I could hear her smug shadow talking through her. She told me how her friend had visited the night before, how she'd brought beers and a pizza and ice cream, 'And you know what,' she said, kidding herself as well as me, 'I could take it or leave it.' She was telling me that she was proud of the fact that she could look her old nemesis in the eye and not be tempted. 'But you still took it?' I asked rhetorically. I already knew the answer. 'Well, yeah,' she said, 'but that's the point. I didn't even enjoy it.' I heard shadow and I warned her, but she didn't hear. Within a very short time she was back on the junk again (saying 'I can take it or leave it' as she gorged) and her three stone plus a stone more for good measure came back with a vengeance. I am happy to say that this splendid lady (only after some time and much effort) did find her purpose again, and is currently back on the path.

As I said, now's the time to begin, make finding purpose your purpose, and the moment your purpose becomes clear, act. Do not err, do not put it off, do not try and find a better time to start; that window of opportunity, the portal that all your effort has opened, the wormhole to the next dimension that you have worked so hard to create will close again in a heartbeat if you don't take advantage and climb through. To reopen it you will have to start all over again. Each portal that you open to a new dimension is bespoke; it is a couture passageway created uniquely by and specifically for you. It will never be there again in the same way, so use it or lose it.

Now that we have established the importance of purpose and the power that purpose lends us, it's time to make an inventory of all our known shadows, so that we can clear ourselves of them and open ourselves up to a bigger and better universe.

Before creating the inventory proper, this might be a good time to get rid of anything and everything in your life that is weighing you down, because from here on in you are going to need energy, and as much as you can get, so if there is anything in your life that is stealing your energy, now is the time to let it go. Now is the time to lighten the load.

Lightening the load

If you want to take a journey across a heady terrain – and walking the left-hand path, the path of the shadow hunter is indeed heady terrain – it really helps if you can lighten the load before you set off. Cut the fat from your life, tick off those overdue jobs, delegate the things that can be better completed by somebody else, and completely let go of the to-do jobs that you neither want nor intend to do. Unfinished business creates stress, because while they are not being completed you're carrying them. It takes a lot less energy to actually do a job, or delegate a job or dump a job, than it does to carry it around in your body for weeks, months or even years. Lighten the load and do it now. If you don't then the load becomes a shadow, just another redundant, squatting demon feeding off your life energy. You need your life energy to live and create; you don't want to waste your life energy on anti-life, and anything you're carrying that's not serving a positive purpose is anti-life. So make the strong decision and get rid of it. Make the list. Make it now. It can be scary because you might find that the list includes things you didn't even know you wanted to get rid of. You might suddenly realise that you're in the wrong job, or that you are holding on to influences that no longer serve, or perhaps even that you're living in entirely the wrong life.

On one of my recent six-month masterclass sessions we had a lovely man who came along (he thought) to learn self defence. On the first session I told him and the rest of the class that the first lesson in self defence is defence against the self. And part of self defence against the self is drawing up a list of the things in your life that are no longer serving you. Now this was a successful man. He was a journalist on one of the top newspapers in the world, and up until that point he thought this was where he wanted to be, where he was meant to be, even where he was destined to be. By the third session he realised two very important things: 1) He was working in the wrong employ. What he really wanted to do, what he'd always had a passion for, was broadcasting. He'd always wanted to run a radio station, but up until that point he'd never really taken his desire seriously. He thought (like many) that work had to be something you hated; it couldn't be something that you actually loved doing. 2) He realised that he didn't want to learn self defence after all; what he really wanted to do was clear this bubble of fear that was constantly sitting just below the surface of his skin. Initially he thought that learning to be a good fighter on a self defence course might help him to do that. Now he knew differently. So he left the course (my job was done) and he left his employ as an international journalist to run his own radio station, which he is still doing to this day.

Similarly, when I first decided to become a shadow hunter and lighten my own load I discovered lots of things that up until that time were unknown to me. One of them was my then partner! It is so hard to say this, and it is even harder to place it in print because she was (and she still is) a great girl, she was just not a great girl for me. And back then I was terrified of even admitting it to myself, let alone announcing it to the world. But I was ill at the time, I had just gone through a massive depression (or what I call a massive purification period) and I knew that if I did not write a completely honest list I would find myself back in the same sorry mess in a year's time. So she went on the list, as did other members of my family and friends who pulled me down. They say that you can choose your friends but you can't choose your family. I disagree. You perhaps can't choose the fact that they are your family, but you can choose whether or not you keep them as influences. You don't have to hang around with people who are terrible to you or who destroy your sense of self-worth just because they're family; you have to look at them as individual souls and recognise that even though you may have started the journey with them, you certainly don't have to finish it together. I see families destroy each other all the time, and still come back for more, because they think they have to, because blood is thicker than water.

Things that no longer serve, things that hold you back, things that take more from you than they give, things and people that are redundant: get rid of them and you will be so light that you'll probably float up and hit the ceiling. Your energy levels will multiply, and your vision will be clearer than you could ever believe. I will go into this in greater detail in the next chapter.

You have access to anything you want in the world. Anything: all the ideas, the innovations, the money, the fame, the house, the car, the health, the perfect partner, the wealth, God. This abundance is all around you now, as we speak, ready to be plucked from the sky and placed into your swag bag, but your vision of these riches is being blocked by shadow. This is why cleaning your life of all and any shadow is so important. Each time you dissolve a shadow, overcome a fear and face your demons, you will get a little more access to your own personal lottery.

Lightening the load is one of the first steps in working on the internal shadow. And it's very necessary because it'll free up vital energy, and in this game you will need all the power you can find.

Chapter 7

The Shadow Inventory

This is the time to make an inventory of all your known, external fears (shadows, sub-personalities) and prepare to hunt them down. This takes a great deal of self-honesty and self-knowledge. It also takes courage, or should I say it develops courage. And it is uncomfortable. But *anabolic discomfort* is where you develop an internal physique. It is where you find hardiness.

Grab yourself a piece of paper and a pen. Sit down somewhere quiet, where you know you won't be disturbed or interrupted. Write down all the things in the physical world that you feel frightened of. Be brutally honest. No one else is going to see this list; no one else *needs* to see this list. This is important, because there may be things on it that you don't want others to see. At some point you may want to share your list with others, because that may be a part of your process, but for now it's a private affair and it should remain that way. Start with a very wide-ranging list of everything that you find scary, frightening or terrifying in your life. Later we may be able to cross some of the list off, because your fears may be natural, like a fear of man-eating tigers. Or your fear may be impotent, in that it is so weak it doesn't really affect your life. I'm really interested in the juicy stuff, the fears that are debilitating, the fears that stop you from doing with your life what you would really like to do. If you struggle with addictions – food, drink, drugs – include them on your list. While you may not immediately associate them with fears or shadows, they are the worst kind. If you are overweight, for instance, and you can't make yourself eat healthily, then you have a very large, debilitating shadow right there. Have a look at your alcohol consumption. Most people think that they're moderate drinkers, but many are not; they drink to excess, but call it moderation. If you're unsure about this, try and imagine going without a drink when you go on holiday for a fortnight, or better still go without a drink this weekend, or when you go to the next party (stag do, wedding, funeral, birthday, christening, etc.) you've been invited to. Your reaction to this suggestion will give an indication of where you stand with regard to drink. If you feel indignant or angry or defensive at the suggestion of abstinence then the chances are your habit is attached to a shadow. Don't forget that the only reason we're heading towards external fears is so that we can flush out internal shadows. All external fears lead back to projections from the self. In the *Tao Te Ching* (verse 52) Lau Tsu says, 'to find the origin, trace back the manifestations, when you recognise the children, and find the mother, you will be free of sorrow'. The manifestations are your external fears, the children; once you recognise the children and trace them back you will find the mother, which is the shadow inside you, then you will be able to expose and dissolve it. The shadow inventory is your way of listing all the manifestations in order that you can trace them back to their source.

Let me give you an example. My friend Maya was having problems in her life with relationships. When she met a man and started a liaison everything would be fine and dandy, but once the relationship became established she started to experience problems. She would make plans to go out for the day with her new man and then, at the very last moment, and for no apparent reason, she would cancel. She wasn't even sure herself why she did this, only that a tremendous fear arose in her at the very last moment, and the fear overwhelmed her to the point that wild horses wouldn't drag her out of the house. It upset her as much as it upset her partners, who would often be infuriated. And rightly so; often the plans had been set for weeks, even months. Money had been spent, tickets bought, arrangements made to meet friends, and sometimes even flights and hotels had been booked. But once Maya had made her mind up that she wasn't going, nothing could convince her to change it back again. She ended up falling out with a lot of people because of it. As far as she was concerned she'd just changed her mind, and that was her prerogative, and anyone who said she was being unreasonable or tried to talk her out of her decision were in her eyes (and in her words) just bullies, which made her dig her heels in even more. Her partners would try and talk her round and convince her that she should go and that she would have a great time, some of them even begged her to be reasonable, but it just seemed to make her worse. This kind of coercing simply fed her decision to stand her ground (it fed her shadow). This came to a head (as these things do) when she finally met a man who didn't buy into her drama, and when at the very last minute she said 'I'm not going!' he simply said, 'OK, don't go. I'll go on my own.' And he did, again and again. In fact in the end he wouldn't go on his own, he would ring a friend and say, 'I am going to so-and-so for the day. Maya has decided not to go, so do you want to come with me?' And he would take someone else instead. This was a shock to Maya, who was used to getting a big reaction when she changed plans at the last minute. It really made her think, and it made her look at her life. Not least because suddenly for the first time she found herself with someone that she really cared for. She could see there was a real danger that, if she didn't sort herself out, she might lose him. She went to talk with a spiritual adviser, who recognised that Maya's antics were the manifestations of a shadow, and he helped her to trace it back. It turned out that as a teenager Maya was an amazing runner, destined for the national arena. She was invited to try out for her regional squad, and very naturally she was nervous. Right before the big day she got more and more tense, and with no one to speak to, an older head perhaps who might have told her that her anticipation was quite natural and that everyone feels nerves, she allowed the anticipation to become a fully fledged fear. So she tentatively approached her running coach, quite a stern disciplinarian, and told her that she was thinking about pulling out of the trials. Rather than talk to Maya and reassure her and encourage her to face her fears, the coach instead told her that she had to go to the trials, she was booked in; the school was relying on her so she had no choice. This just made Maya feel ten times worse. She dug her heels in and, at the very last moment, pulled out of the run. The teacher was livid, Maya was upset, and she never ran competitively again. This was the mother of her problem; this was the root cause of her issues. Once she realised where the trouble started she was able to work on her shadow and release it. She was able to see that her partners were not her old running coach, trying to bully her into doing something that she didn't want to do, and that reliving this school scenario over and again in her adult life was just perpetuating the problem. It was actually growing her shadow. So the next time she was booked to go on a trip or a date or a day out with her partner and she felt the fearful instinct to cancel all plans and lock the doors, she overrode her fear and went. And each time she did this her unnatural compulsion weakened the shadow until eventually it was completely dissolved.

Find the mother, find the cure.

Back to the shadow inventory. Make the list, be thorough, leave no stone unturned, be brave, put everything down, make the list long, make it exhaustive: it will be very exciting when you get to the hunting part of the equation and you start crossing those shadows off. Let me tell you something interesting: when you sit down on your own and start this process, aware of the fact that it's secret and private and that no one else will see your list, and so you will not be outed or judged, you might be surprised at two things. 1) Fears will appear on your list that you may not have been consciously aware of. My first list contained a fear of spiders, a fear of the dentist, a fear of karate competitions and a fear of... my partner! I didn't expect that, not in a million years. I was writing away and it just suddenly added itself to my list. It was a shock, I have to say. But then, when I looked at it, I thought, 'Yeah, that's about right, I am scared of her.' She was a strong girl, and she was dominant. She was gorgeous, but she was a very governing woman, and as we all know dominance can very quickly spill into bullying. But the problem was not in my partner. She was the manifestation, the child. The mother (the cause) was in me. This was easy to trace back (it came from a strict Catholic upbringing and a strong mum) and easy, in theory, to treat. I just started to stand up for myself. This inclusion on my list, when traced back, had a root cause: I was the third brother in my family, the youngest boy, and I had been spoiled. I was given a lot of love and I was protected by everyone; I was led by everyone (and all for the right reasons, even if it did turn out wrong) and because of that I never really learned to self-lead. When I got together with my first serious partner she became an extension of my family, and she led me as they had led me. And I let her, because I was so used to it. I just allowed it to carry forward, thinking that it was entirely normal. That is until I became frightened of standing up for myself, and I allowed myself to be dominated. As a boy this was OK because I was young, I had no responsibilities, but as a man this behaviour left me feeling weak and unprepared for the harsh realities of making a living and raising a family. My partner had done nothing wrong really, she had just picked up the baton and run with it. She'd simply developed a masculinity to counterbalance my obvious shortfall, and this made me a poor excuse for a man. Looking back I can also see that, because I let her dominate, she had absolutely no respect for me at all and it showed in her increasingly hostile behaviour, to the point that she would brag to her friends (overheard, very upsetting) that when she said 'Jump!' I said 'How high?' That saddened me, so she ended up on my list and I started to assert myself a little more and began to redress the balance. This caused problems, as you can imagine. She was so used to getting her own way that when I suddenly started to challenge her she kicked off, and arguments, cold dinners and a cold back in bed became the norm for quite a while. Shadows that are this established do not go without a fight. Eventually we split up, and it was painful, but we are both better and happier people because of it now. This doesn't have to be the case, of course; many people manage to get through marital problems and live happily ever after.

The second thing that often happens – and this is a lovely revelation – is that the very act of placing your shadow on paper often dissolves it. This is especially so for the surface shadows, those that are hitching a ride and not knitted into your very fibre. This was the case with me when I wrote down my fear of dentists (which traced back to a very bad experience I had when I was a boy). The moment I wrote it down and looked at it, I thought, How ridiculous. I booked an appointment with the dentist (first time in ten years), went down, had some treatment and was never fearful of dentists again. The shadow was out the moment I wrote it down.

Another interesting thing is this: sometimes clearing one shadow can wipe out a whole battalion of smaller shadows in one go. When I gave up alcohol, for instance, lots and lots of other smaller shadows (including some shadow friends) were instantly dissolved. Giving up drink after a lifetime of having a tipple was very hard for me, an Everest of a challenge. But once I did it, all those little hills that I usually struggled to climb were easy by comparison. In fact, they didn't even need climbing any more, because they no longer represented a challenge to me.

I had a great fear of giving up alcohol. It never felt like a fear at first; drinking just felt like an ordinary, acceptable pastime. But when I tried giving it up (my brother had died from alcoholism, and I decided that it would be a healthy exercise in cerebral hardiness to abstain), I couldn't do it. The thought of never having a drink again, ever, caused a lot of discomfort in me and a lot of sadness. It soon became clear why. When I traced this 'child' back and found the mother I realised that this was not simply about giving up alcohol, this was about giving up an identity. I had been brought up with alcohol, everyone I knew liked 'the drink' (and the drink liked them), and all my social relationships revolved around drinking, I didn't know a single person who didn't partake – it was in the flesh and bones of my life. One of the big occasions of my youth was becoming a member of the local working men's club. It was almost like an initiation; when I got my membership book (complete with Ladies Card) I became a man! Even after I packed in drinking and the working men's club fell outside of my orbit, my dad still renewed my card every year until I became a life member. It was very important, he said. 'You never know when you might be passing and want to pop in.' So giving up drinking meant no longer leaning on the bar with my dad and my brothers. It meant I was no longer the Geoff who had a pint and talked bollocks and got pissed with his mates at the weekend. I was suddenly the Geoff that didn't drink. And that made me ever so different in the world I came from. In one fell swoop, and with something as little as giving up alcohol, I launched myself into an entirely new orbit. I knew there was no way I could stop drinking and it not have a domino of effects on every other aspect of my life. And, of course, it did. I lost many of my mates, my whole social circle changed, I changed. And for the better. I spoke with a young guy about this yesterday actually. He was thinking of giving up drink but he didn't want to lose his friends. I offered him the advice that I'll offer you: if you lose a friend because you decide to no longer drink alcohol, they were not much of a friend in the first place. The people who are very important in your life will stay with you no matter what you do.

So this one fear, once overcome, widened my perspective to such an extent that I felt like I could achieve anything. I felt so powerful that lots of lesser fears that were hiding inside me vacated immediately. The light that shone into me after losing this shadow dissolved a multitude of others.

Remember when doing this exercise that every excess in your life is feeding a shadow and so should go on your list. If you were not afraid of it, or not afraid of not having it, you'd have overcome it by now, so write it down.

Put the shadows in order, place your least feared at the bottom and your most feared at the top. And be prepared to keep adding to the list as you go along, because other shadows, ones that were previously hidden, will present themselves en route. I've found that shadows are often stacked or layered on top of each other, and because of this not all of them are visible. As you dissolve the shadows that are on top, the ones below suddenly appear. So they should go on your list too.

Some will dissolve in the beat of your heart, a few may take a lifetime to get rid of, and a small minority might stay the whole incarnation. The latter (and any of the long-term shadows that will not vacate immediately) can be yoked and used as energy (giving your vices voices). As long as you can control the force, you can use the energy for good. As I said earlier you can strip the label from your shadow, draw the energy and make something beautiful by transmuting it. This method of siphoning off the shadow bit by bit takes understanding, it takes self-control and it takes courage – all of which you will develop as you go. You have to respect the shadow, because like electricity it can damage you if underestimated even for a second. But as I've already stated, no one said this was going to be easy – we are not in the game of easy – this is the game of hard.

If you are not entirely sure of all the things you're afraid of it might be better to look at all the aspects of your life that you are not happy with; this will give you a clearer indication. If you are not happy with your job, why haven't you left your job and changed it for a better one, or better still invested time and money in yourself and become more employable? There are shadows abundant here. When I was stuck in the factory I thought (and I told myself) that I was kept there by the will of my partner. Actually I was stuck there because I was scared to leave; change meant temporary discomfort and a new identity and I was afraid of that. Writing down my shadow inventory and tracing back my fears to their core also showed me that, at the time, I didn't think myself worthy of a better-paid job, so I began working on building my esteem, challenging myself to be a better man, educating myself through the library, questioning myself and those around me, and questioning the society-imposed and self-imposed rules that kept me in my place. I earned a higher esteem by doing heroic things (and challenging the norm is always heroic). Confidence comes from doing difficult things, and the more difficult they are the more confident you will become, and when you are confident, changing jobs becomes no more difficult than changing suits.

Are you in the wrong body? Is your body out of shape? Is it undernourished? Is it addicted? Is it ill? If so, then all of these things represent a fear which in turn is linked to a shadow. If you get yourself into shape, if you nourish yourself and kill your addictions and in the process make it your life's purpose to be healthy, you will dissolve major shadows and place yourself head and shoulders above the norm.

These are big fears, these are major shadows and they represent real challenge, but the rewards for overcoming them are huge. You would need to develop self-sovereignty to do this, and very few people ever develop self-sovereignty, even though it is available to all.

Changing frequencies

How about your influences? Are you happy with them? Did you know that your influences are the best indicator of where and who you are right now? We attract who and what we are. So if you want to know who and what you are, just look around you and see a mirror reflection. If the influences that surround you (especially if they are very close, like a spouse or a best mate) are not inspiring, then it's time to change your influences, and the best way to do that is to change you. Imagine you are tuned in to a frequency and that all your influences share the same wavelength. The frequency you hold represents your orbit. If you don't like these influences, twiddle the dial and change it for a better one. If the frequency is not inspirational, if it is not encouraging and if is not uplifting, then, like the master archer that misses the target, we should always look to ourselves for the cause of error.

I had a friend who was manic depressive. That's the frequency he was tuned into. He told me that he was surrounded by depressed people that pulled him down, belittled him, bullied him and even violently attacked him. His wife took drugs, his friends too, and together they would sit around all day, every day, and talk about how dark and conspiratorial the world was. Theirs was a collective frequency. My friend blamed his influences for keeping him depressed. I told him that he could 'disappear' the whole lot of them simply by changing wavelengths. This would be easy enough. All he had to do was change everything he ingested from junk to healthy and everything he did from disempowering to empowering. I told him, 'I could show you how to do that.' He believed me; I know he did because he suddenly got scared. If he changed his frequency, what would that mean in practical terms? What would he lose? He might lose his wife (after all you can't *make* people change with you, you can't change their frequency for them, they have to do that themselves) he might lose many of his friends, it would probably mean changing his geographic location, in other words finding somewhere else to live and finding a different way to live… Actually it meant becoming an entirely different person. This saddened him (and at the same time it excited him) because as much as he hated being depressed and as much as he was tired of the kind of garbage life he was living he did love these people, and he did feel safe in the world he inhabited, even if it was a sad life. He found himself with a decision to make. He knew there was little chance of his wife and friends coming with him, he knew them well enough to know that, and he felt a lot of guilt, as though perhaps getting himself better would mean abandoning the people he loved, leaving them behind. I explained to him that you don't abandon anyone, you just follow your own path and they follow theirs, and you never leave people behind, some of them just chose not to come with you. If, out of some sort of twisted loyalty, you did stay for the sake of your friends and family, you wouldn't be helping them in the least. Spiritually speaking, you would just be perpetuating their problem, and you would not be helping yourself either, just holding yourself back. The only way you can really help other people who are trapped is by making a way out for yourself, and in the process showing them that it can be done, in the hope that if and when they are ready they will take the journey too. My friend had built up such a strong internal support system for his shadows that it had spilled out into the world, where he was surrounded by other lost souls that acted as prison bars around his self constructed jail. He knew that his world was shrinking – that's why he sought me out in the first place – and he also knew that if he didn't get out now he might die at the frequency he was holding. So he took my advice, and he started to change his frequency very gradually by changing himself, and one by one his old friends fell out of the orbit, and eventually his wife fell out of his orbit too. He desperately tried to encourage them to go with him, he begged them to change, and he passed on the lessons he'd learned in the hope that they would be inspired as he had been inspired, but to no avail. Eventually, as they realised how determined he was to get well, they started to shun him, accusing him of changing and of abandoning them and of trying to be something bigger than (they thought) he was. So he had to let them go. He got better. He changed himself and changed his life. Of course, he found a whole new band of friends, people in a higher frequency, people who aspired to live an authentic life, like him. And later he got back to work, fell in love and got married again, to a beautiful girl who he met in his new frequency. And today he lives a fruitful and happy life. He has his challenges like the rest of us, but he knows that if things are not right he can change them by changing himself.

I also know lots of people who have changed frequency, and those closest to them have changed with them. Often people will come with you, but remember that is their choice and not yours.

Scrutinise your whole life. Lay it out on the page and take a good hard look at it and see what does and what does not fit. When I looked at my own life in my mid-twenties I didn't really like much of what of what I saw there. I'm not saying that I wasn't ever happy because I was; you adjust. But I was not consistently happy. I was not authentically happy. I knew that I could do better. I knew that I could be better than I was. I was working in a menial job that I hated and I didn't feel contented in my marriage. I was training in martial arts at the time, but only recreationally; I really dreamed of becoming a full-time teacher. My social life was based around alcohol and was very uninspiring; it was completely bereft of culture and I so wanted to be inspired. I desperately wanted to become a professional writer, but felt that I lacked the ability, the know-how and the opportunity, and becoming a writer was so far outside of my orbit that I felt it was about as likely as a Euromillions Lottery win. I was very unhappy in my own skin. I had a beautiful body, but had no control at all over its impulses and its desires, and certainly none over its fears. I was a man living in entirely the wrong world and not brave enough, not intelligent enough and not wise enough to change it for one that better suited. And I felt that my cowardice was an insult. I didn't like myself very much at all. In the mirror I saw a lot of self-loathing staring back at me. The only thing that I did love, and I loved with all my heart, was my babies. My children were everything to me. But that was also a source of angst because I didn't feel as though I was teaching them to live the kind of amazing life that I knew was available to them, because I was not living it myself.

So you can imagine, when I wrote my list of fears it was exhaustive.

Once the list was written, I traced each fear back to its root, and then I went out to hunt those shadows down.

This leads us nicely to the main thrust of this book, 'hunting the shadow'.

You may have realised by now that you are already hunting and dissolving shadows; you have been from the moment you picked this book up. Just the act of buying these pages and reading them means that you are in the arena. Merely looking for information on self-development is shadow hunting. Working on the body and clearing it of fear and residue and addiction and negative influences *is* shadow hunting. Building your will by placing it to work in the power triune *is* shadow hunting. Lightening the load is also an exercise in hunting and dissolving shadow, and making a shadow inventory means that you are in the hunt proper, right up to your neck. So in the next chapter we will look at specific exercises for hunting shadow, but bear in mind – as I said – that you are already on the path (so congratulations!).

Chapter 8

Hunting the Shadow

Hunting shadow is easy in principle, once you have your list. Start at the bottom with your smallest fears, seek them out and face them, and in facing them you will dissolve the root. If your fear is of going to the dentist, go to the dentist, and keep going until you no longer fear it. In principle it is no more difficult than that. If your fear is of being assertive, start to practise being assertive with people who step over the line with you, and when the discomfort arises sit in it. That place of discomfort is delicious, it's like fertiliser; it'll grow you like nothing else. Even if you're sitting at home contemplating facing down a fear, your indecision, that place between *Should I?* and *Shouldn't I?* will develop your internal game. If there is no discomfort in your life there is no growth in your life. To take yourself to a better place you need to develop yourself into a better person, and this is done in the forge of discomfort. So when you feel in turmoil it is important that you remind yourself of this fact. The burn is where the growth is. It is supposed to be hard, it is supposed to be uncomfortable, and only in facing this discomfort will you grow a character. Your spine is moulded by difficulty.

When you're going through the list – sitting at the dentist, asserting yourself, running a marathon, going for a better job, doing a presentation at work, losing weight, training – don't allow yourself to complain about the fact that it hurts. It is supposed to hurt, and you just have to learn to like the fact that it hurts. In fact, you have to learn to love the fact that it hurts, knowing that the discomfort of dissolving your sub-personalities is where your success and your freedom lies. If you don't remember this, if you don't remind yourself, you'll fall into the trap of feeling needlessly tortured and give up. Don't give up. Anyone can give up and you are not anyone.

Each time you expose a shadow and overcome a fear your courage and your wisdom will grow, which makes each subsequent challenge easier than the last. You need to get a list of successful encounters behind you. That is why it is important to start facing and overcoming the smaller fears first; it will grow your confidence. Some of your shadows will disappear very quickly, perhaps even after one exposure, while others might take three of four exposures and some can take years, but that's OK. You (like me) are a work in progress. No matter how slowly (even at a snail's pace), you must keep moving forwards. If you find that you reach a sticking point with a shadow and you can't seem to find your way past, take the sting out of the tail by talking to (or reading about) other people who have dissolved a similar shadow. This will make your quest feel more achievable. Or flood yourself with information about the fear in question to weaken it. Knowledge dispels fear.

Shadows will out. That much has been established thus far: they will out, with or without your help. These trapped emotions, learned habits, developed or inherited internal demons and borrowed shadows have no place inside a balanced, healthy human being. They cause internal chaos leading to illness and, if left to their own devices, internal and external anarchy, even death.

Situations will arise in your life (or you can deliberately create situations) that will act as a poultice to draw out, expose and dissolve hidden, internal shadows that might be blocking your growth.

The shadow poultice

Something as simple as buying an expensive car can draw out a vanity shadow like a poultice. For three years I drove a Jaguar XKR, which really drew the ego and vanity out of me. In fact, I smashed the car up twice (vanity crashes, as I called them) because I was so busy revelling in the admiring glances that I failed to heed the traffic, and crashed. This was an expensive exercise for me, but it proved to be worth its weight in gold. The second crash cost me about £4,000 and a lot of hassle. It took me a month to get the car fixed. I had been driving out of a car park, noticed a good-looking girl eying my vehicle and while I was busy bathing in her admiring glances I drove straight through some parking posts and wrecked the front of the car. It jarred me so much that a shadow jumped out of me and I felt this sudden rush of disproportionate guilty terror. I felt embarrassed and ashamed and very low. A part of me felt overwhelmed by the situation and I could feel panic racing through my whole body. I wanted to cry. This (I have to tell you emphatically) is not me. Not the real me. I am a man who has faced life-threatening violence on a regular basis and I have fronted terrifying ordeals in my life and held my nerve, so panicking over a broken car was definitely a sub-personality (that I did not even know I had) and not the real me. As soon as I recognised that this panicking shadow was not me, that it was not who I am and that it was an old shadow, I was able to get to work. What I found very interesting here is the fact that my shadow was throwing a million guilt trips at me because of the crash and yet I knew that if it had been my wife who'd crashed the car I'd have been fine with it. I wouldn't have batted an eyelid, and I certainly would not have attacked her (like I was attacking myself) and told her what an incompetent idiot she was. This enabled me to realise that the sub-vocalising and guilty part of me was shadow, and the moment I recognised this I separated myself (my true self) from this shadow and over the next few weeks while my car was being fixed and I was trying to sort out the insurance I processed this shadow by focusing on it every time it reared its head. When I say focus I mean that I went into the very centre of the feeling, and I sat there. I killed the story (which was talking about guilt, expense, shame and embarrassment) because I knew that the story was feeding the shadow, so I starved the shadow and within a short time I was able to let the shadow go completely. (I will explain more about 'the story' and how to kill the story later.)

The inhospitable host

You can force out shadows by making yourself an inhospitable host. When I had a disabling fear of violence I became a nightclub doorman, which forced out my shadow, very quickly, because my life became inhospitable for the part of me that was terrified. When I had a greed shadow, I deliberately changed my diet and ate very light; this forced and starved my shadow out. When I was addicted to alcohol I deliberately abstained from drinking in order to hunt, expose and dissolve the shadow. Whatever your shadow feeds off, whether it is jealousy or junk food, people-pleasing or sexual pornography, starve them of their sustenance and you will become an inhospitable host.

Shadow enticement

You can entice your shadow out by exposing yourself to the things it lusts for, and then dissolve it the moment it comes out to play. Be careful with this one, though, if you are dealing with strong, established shadows because it can backfire. It is an advanced technique that can go wrong if you have not developed massive self-control. I had a friend that used this technique by deliberately watching strong sexual pornography to draw out a shadow, but because at the time his will was not as strong as his shadow, he found himself more addicted than before.

My dad also used this technique successfully with tobacco. When he wanted to quit smoking he carried a pack of cigarettes around with him everywhere, and every time he had the urge to smoke, he'd lock on to that urge (the shadow), and by sitting in the centre of the feelings and killing the story he was able to dissolve it.

Shadow trickery

When I ran a full-time martial arts club I employed trickery to draw people's shadows out. I'd tell my students that we were going to have an easy class in the next session, and then when they arrived I'd shock them with a very hard fighting class. This would always trick out their shadow; even some of the veteran fighters faced suddenly with a knock-out or submission class would tremble, become monosyllabic and fearful of carrying on. This was not them, this was their shadow, and the moment their shadow came out I would get them to sit in the feelings, kill the story and release the shadow. This kind of exposure also developed internal hardiness. All the people who trained diligently with me through that period became impressively strong individuals.

Reaction formation

You can also 'mirror' out shadows; when you catch yourself looking at someone and judging their worst attributes, especially if you find them particularly offensive, you're seeing a mirror image of your own shadow reflecting back at you. In psychology they call this Reaction Formation; we hate in others what we most dislike in ourselves. The key with mirroring is that it allows us to see everyone as our teacher; what we hate most in them is what we hate most in us. The moment we recognise this, we should break off from our judgement, recognise that our shadow is out and lock onto it and, once locked on, dissolve it with strong focus.

There are other methods that bring out shadow that I am not expert in, but I'll outline them here in the hope that you might look them up and take some expert instruction. T'ai chi and qigong are excellent for clearing shadow, because they are methods of moving and clearing energy, especially trapped energy, through, around and out of the chakras. Chanting is also great for clearing out shadows; the sound vibration jars trapped energy free and helps in the process of clearing the body of residue. I experienced a sound bath recently given by a wonderful woman called Helen Braithwaite (www.soundsintuitive.co.uk) and I found it to be an incredibly potent form of shadow shifting, I experienced sensations and visions and releases of trapped energy that I never thought possible from just one session. The beauty of sound baths is that they completely bypass the rational conscious self, and go deep into body and mind. It felt to me like a psychic enema, clearing residues of energy that were trapped.

These are different ways in which you can hunt and clear your trapped energy, your shadow, so while I am advocating here that we all go out and hunt our shadows down (and I am advocating that), I am also saying that life is offering you the opportunity every day to clear shadow. If your shadow represents a scarcity mentality (you believe that there is not enough to go around, and so you become greedy and hoard your wealth) then life may place someone or something (a situation) in front of you to encourage and develop your generosity. The way to overcome a scarcity mentality and prove that there is abundance in the universe is to defy your greedy shadow and court generosity. You may have an abandonment schema, that perhaps has manifested itself as a jealousy shadow for example, and you suddenly find that your husband wants to get involved in a social group that does not involve you. This is life offering you the chance to go with the situation and draw out your shadow. Or perhaps you have a deep-seated shadow that is afraid of being publicly ridiculed (one of my friends had this and the fear made her world very small and very scary), and suddenly at work you are asked to do a presentation in front of some visiting clients. This, again, is the universe serving up an opportunity for you to face your fear and clear your shadow once and for all.

And life will always and continually do this until you oust all of your sub-personalities and become one. Or, as it says in *The Aquarian Gospel of Jesus* (chapter 2, verse 9), God will 'level down the hills and fill the valleys up'.

Every situation that is offered and not engaged, or not seen through to the bitter end, will have to be undergone again and again and the same emotions and the same discomforts experienced until you do see it through.

In my early life I ran away from shadow and I ran away from fear, and when I did the fear and the shadow grew. The faster and the more frequently and urgently and frightfully I ran, the quicker and the bigger my shadow became. I recognised this process very early on and I could sense a benevolent force in the universe that was trying to show me that my happiness and my joy and my treasure were not in that no-man's-land that I kept running to (and never finding). Rather, my freedom lay somewhere through and beyond the shadow that I was running from. And if I would only stop for a second, if I could only turn and at least face my fears, I would get all the assistance in the world. Seen and unseen forces would appear miraculously and help me overcome those fears.

The chickpea

In a poem by Rumi (called 'The Chickpea'), the chickpea is being boiled alive in a pot of water, and he keeps trying to climb out, but the chef keeps pushing him back in with his ladle. The chickpea feels needlessly tormented. The chef smiles and says to the chickpea, 'You think I'm torturing you. I'm not torturing you; I am just trying to make you sweet so that you can sit with the rice and the herbs.' As soon as the chickpea realises that his torment is not needless he says to the chef, 'Push me in twice, because I can't do this by myself.'

You may find that life proffers a situation that will 'out' a shadow. You may bump into it, trip over it, you may find yourself waking up one morning and the shadow is there waiting for you on the pillow in the form of depression or fear or dread, it may be staring out at you from your breakfast cereal. A job promotion may trigger an old insecurity shadow; a health issue may force you to assess the way you are living your life; an acrimonious divorce might be asking you to take a closer look at who you are. There are always opportunities to clear your shadows, even though those opportunities might not initially be very welcome when they come. My experience informs me that everything has divinity in it, everything that happens to us is meant and every single thing that happens to us is good.

But waiting for situations to befall us and then trying to fight from the back foot can be a disempowering way to live. You are fighting from a defensive position, which is always more tiring. It is better, I think, to be pre-emptive and engage your fears now, rather than wait and have to dig yourself out of some cesspit of a situation.

Hunt it down, face it down, and dissolve it.

You have your list, your shadow inventory, so you are ready to go.

The moment you initiate this kind of adventure you will start to notice things in your life that you never noticed before. You will become more aware of your surroundings and your influences, and your own reactions to your surroundings and influences, and how much you are controlled (like a machine) by the pressure that both of them place on you to conform to the norm. You will realise how little freedom most people really have, and you will see that your jailer is fear. You'll eventually recognise and accept, through diligent introspection and self honesty, that all the fear is in you. You are your own beginning, middle and end. And you will become very excited when you also realise that you can dissolve that fear and find your freedom whenever you want to. If you want to see the state of your (or any person's) energy or the nature of your shadows, just look at the world in which you live, and the people (and the things) that surround you, it will give you a clear indication of what is going on inside.

Normally when the shadows are established and dominant you will see projections all around you that represent the state of your internal schematic. Not always immediately, sometimes when people are very conniving (or should I say their shadows are conniving) it can take a while for those manifestations to show up. Recently a priest in a backwater town in England was convicted of gross indecency towards children, and imprisoned. He is currently surrounded by what can only be described as an inferno of dark and depraved archetypes, all of which fully represent his internal shadows. And yet for years he was able to keep his perversions secret, and stop, temporarily, the manifestations of those shadows from projecting into his reality. His congregation had no idea that he was a practising paedophile, with perverted photographs of naked children adorning the walls of every private room in his rectory. Even after he was convicted and publicly humiliated they were still in shock. He kept his perversions very close to his chest.

This is unusual, and normally the sign of very big and very dominant shadows, perhaps even demonic shadows, or shadows that have completely possessed the person.

Normally shadows feed off us, if they are strong they may partly possess us, and if they are fully established and integrated into our software, then they can actually become us. The latter (as in the case of the priest) is the exception and not the norm, and even then it is not too late to clear them out. Usually the world in which a person lives is a major indicator of the shadows that inhabit them. If you see someone sat at a table full of gangsters, or violent people, or criminals, then you're seeing his innards on full display. As within, as without. Similarly, you usually see depressed people surrounded by other depressed people, ill people knocking around with other ill people, while cynics and gossips get their heads together all the time. Violent people are always either with other violent people or with weak people who act as their followers. And their surroundings will usually also represent their inner state. When I was stuck in a violent frequency all of my friends were either equally violent, or they were followers of (what they perceived to be) my strength. My house was a cavern of violence, with weapons stationed in every room, even the smallest room, and books about violence and violent people decorating every empty surface and shelf. The people that came into my life who were not of the same ilk did not stay long.

So it will not be hard for you as a hunter of shadows to know where to start when the hunt begins.

The idea of finding your external fear shadows is to expose them, and in doing so develop desensitisation to the feelings of fear that they elicit. This process is cleansing and it also develops cerebral hardiness. Shadow hunters are warriors. You have to develop a lot of courage to face your demons, even if they are only demons of your own making. As I said earlier, start by clearing the shit you can see, the stuff that is obvious, the manifestations that are in your face. In my case this meant sacking my job as a bouncer, which immediately took me outside the orbit of my strongest and most seductive influences. I threw all the weapons I owned in the bin, I pulled all of my violent books off their shelves and took them down the tip and I ceased training in violent arts. I stopped working on the martial aspect of the combat arts that I was practising and instead concentrated on the art itself. I did not have violent conversations (with myself or with others) or allow myself to project into angry (internal or external) diatribes about what I would do to this person or that person if they attacked me or threatened me or my family. I simply did not allow my mind to go there. This placed a vacuum around me that killed the oxygen of all my negative influences, and this allowed my true element to glow. In my art I sought perfection of the self through perfection of physical technique. We are humans and we are in a corporeal coil, so everything has to be accessed and experienced through the physical. I also took what I had learned in martial arts and naturally allowed it to expand into new, non-martial realities. The courage, the tenacity, the skills, the work ethic, the empathy, the intelligence and the curiosity that I had developed through hard combative training were ideal tools to help me develop myself creatively, intellectually, physiologically, psychologically, morally, ethically, spiritually, economically and environmentally. I took the skills and used them to build myself into a more multidimensional being; I ventured into business, into art, into philosophy and philanthropy, I took the skills into my relationships – I took them into everything – and suddenly my art was no longer about having a fight outside the chip shop on a Friday night, it became about the art of life itself.

So start local. Choose the smallest fears first, approach them, face them continually until the fear has dissipated and use the exposure to build your will. Desensitise yourself to the feelings of fear by starting with small exposures, and know that each external fear you overcome will erase part, if not all of an internal shadow.

Other people's battles

Don't concern yourself too much with the fears of other people at this time. Once others see that you're a shadow hunter and that you are developing a warrior mentality they'll be queuing up to enlist your help, but remember this: they are not your fears, and that is not your quest. You can encourage other people and inspire them to face their fears but, unless they cross with one of your own shadows, leave them do the work themselves and let your actions against your own shadows inspire them into action against theirs. Everyone has their own karma to deal with, and everyone must fight their own battles; you can fight a hundred shadows for your friends and family but it will not help them to grow and it will not lessen their shadow one iota. The only way is through the self. This incarnation is all about self-reliance. If you push weights for other people they will never develop their own physiques. You will never develop courage and they will never develop courage unless courage is called for. This does not mean that you never go to the aid of troubled souls. Of course we must help wherever and whenever we can. What you have to be wary of is that most people don't want you to help them carry their load; they want to give you their load to carry for them. So work diligently and fervently on yourself and know that everything is connected. The very act of dissolving the shadow of one man (you) will start the process of dissolving the shadows of all men.

Killing weeds

Often it is useful to know where the root of a fear lies, but it is not always necessary. What is important is that you find and face the external manifestation until you no longer have any fear of it, and that alone, like a killer of weeds, will eventually find a path through the leaves and the stem and make its way to the source and kill the roots.

I've noticed when I tend my garden that weeds will grow practically anywhere. Give them the tiniest bit of attention in the form of soil and light and liquid and they will grow. Some of the strongest weeds in my garden have managed to find sustenance even in the smallest gap in a slab of concrete, establishing roots that are very difficult to remove. And even when you dig them up, you only have to leave a tiny bit of the root in situ and it will grow all over again. However, if you feed them with weed-killer, it will destroy everything from leaf to root, and it will not be able to grow again, because you have taken away the core. I experimented a little with the weeds in my garden, and I found that if I took away any one element of their substance – light, soil, or water – they died. If I took away all of their sustenance they died very quickly. We know that a weed, or any plant, needs light to grow. So if you upturn a pot and place it on top of the weed, blocking all its access to light, it will not survive. If you stop watering a plant it dies. And of course if you take it out of the soil, it will begin to atrophy immediately. I found this very inspiring because it related so closely to the weeds in my body and mind. Remember the golden rule: what you give attention to will grow, and what you take attention away from will die. Attention is sustenance. It is the very food of weeds. It is the breakfast, dinner and tea of shadows. This, then, is my suggestion: we want and we intend to kill the root of our disabling shadow, but not by digging everything up and hacking it out. Like early surgery this can be clumsy, bloody and dangerous, because all sorts of other things get disturbed and nicked and cut during the process, a bit like using an industrial saw to remove a splinter in your thumb. I've tried this method in the garden and it can be very hit and miss; you only have to leave the tiniest morsel in the soil and the weed will find life again. Locate the fear (and just admitting that you have the fear is locating it) then kill every supply of sustenance it has. Kill the light, kill the water and kill the soil. Give it nothing to feed on and the shadow will die. Not without a bit of kicking and screaming, its natural momentum will allow it a short span of life even without sustenance, but it can't survive (just as nothing can survive) for long without nourishment. And as soon as you kill the feed, flood yourself with (what I call) 'the beautiful poison', or 'high-frequency attention', which acts as a poison to shadow. You will be hitting the shadow, whatever the shadow is, from inside and out.

The beautiful poison

Let me explain to you what 'the beautiful poison' (the high-frequency attention) is. Lower frequencies are depression, melancholy, sadness, hopelessness, anxiety, fear, lust, greed, addiction, judgement, cynicism, violence, etc. And these lower frequencies, what we know as shadows, tend to feed on more of themselves; they attract other shadows that give out the same signals, and they also feed on dense and heavy foods, the junk variety that we are always being advised by health professionals to eschew, and look for relief in the form of instant gratification such as alcohol, drugs, pornography (tabloid, soap, violently stimulating film and music), excess in all its forms, gossip – the usual suspects.

Higher frequency is the poison of shadow; when you pour it over the lower vibrations they dissolve from surface to root. Like household detergents, it kills all known germs dead. Lower-frequency shadows cannot exist in the same place as higher frequencies, any more than darkness can exist when exposed to light. The higher frequencies are readily available to everyone, but they are not delivered free and abundantly to our homes every day like the lower-frequency stuff. You may have to hunt around a bit to find them. When you think about it the lower variety is pretty much shoved down your throat every minute of every hour of every day, in the form of negative and abusive TV programmes, tabloids, magazines (that present themselves as informative and cutting edge, but are really just porn mags in disguise) the dense fast food that's sold cheaply and is made easily available, alcohol (which is not only acceptable but an expected norm) and drug taking (which is now pandemic – even many of our leaders are addicts). Living a clean life is far more the exception than the rule. I'm not saying that this is conspiratorial – I don't think it is maliciously and deliberately directed to harm – I think it's to do with greed and profit (at any expense). I think that it's also to do with ignorance (even some of the most intelligent people still do not get basic cause and effect) and it's related to laziness; people want more with less effort. So what we're being delivered on a daily basis by society is just the lowest common denominator: sex sells, it is easy, so let's sell sex. Junk food sells, it is easy and cheap, so let's sell junk. Negative and abusing TV sells, it is easy and it is cheap to make, so let's make and sell negative and abusive TV. Alcohol sells, it is cheaper than it has ever been, so let's make more alcohol and sell it en masse, let's even make it taste nicer so that we can lure a whole new generation into the use and abuse of drink. There is no deliberate conspiracy, just the literate and semi-literate feeding the ignorant, just the partially sighted (occasionally the fully sighted and abusive) leading the blind.

So you will not be pipe-fed the beautiful poison; you will have to go out there and you will have to find your own supply. And when you do, stop taking in the rubbish that feeds the shadow and start filling yourself with high-frequency material. The high-frequency fare is hope, healthy ambition, courage, curiosity (although apparently this has been known to kill a few cats), motivation, laughter, uplifting music, art and culture, aspiration, inspiration (to be in spirit, to be one with God), charity, anonymous philanthropy, faith, kindness, generosity (a very rare and very high frequency) and, at the very top of the list, love. These are not merely words, they are not simple nouns or empty aphorisms that you tag onto the end of a speech to add a little spice, they are verbs, they are actions, things you do, and if you are a seasoned and holistic human being, they are who you are. Our bodies are constantly vibrating, and when we feel lower emotions, like hate, anger, lust and so on, we are actually vibrating very slowly and we tend to attract other beings and other situations that are vibrating at the same level, like tuning into a radio station by turning the dial to a certain frequency. When we access inspiration, laughter, aspiration and love, we vibrate fast, and at the top end of our game, and similarly we attract like souls, and like situations that are at the same frequency. So if you are vibrating at a low level, you're feeling or experiencing anger for instance, love (when you access love) will completely dissolve it. The anger will disappear like darkness under a spotlight. Love is a metaphysical force that connects you to God, and with it mountains can be moved and seas parted. It is a very powerful frequency, one to work with if you are serious about dissolving shadow. Sub-personalities cannot exist in the presence of light, and love is light.

On a very basic level, love accessed through service will dissolve stress. It will take practice though. To take yourself from the lower vibrations to the higher vibration of love is a big jump, but it can be done. Many times I have felt anger and had the urge to displace it on anyone that gets in my way; I have been able to turn it into pure love by using a combination of knowledge and willpower. I access the knowledge, and remind myself that love is the highest force and that it dissolves every frequency below it, then I utilise my willpower and I embrace the situation that has triggered my shadow. I put my arms around my wife/child/mate and I literally take myself to the higher frequency. I don't always get it right, I am still honing my skills; occasionally I find myself in a bad mood and before I can stop myself I've snapped at someone, or said the wrong thing, or completely lost my temper. This is rare, the times are few and far between, but it happens. We are human, we are learning and to err is a part of the process, so I don't hinder that process by beating myself up afterwards. If I make a mistake, I apologise, usually seconds after the faux pas, and in apologising I take myself once again to the frequency of love.

Apologising when you're wrong is also a way of controlling and slowing down stress. If you don't apologise, you are still carrying the karma of your action, and that tells on the adrenals, which are then on red alert waiting for the inevitable argument that will ensue because of your lack of magnanimity.

Failing to apologise when you know you're in the wrong is also dishonest and it is cowardly, there is no integrity in it, and this is a dark energy that feeds shadow.

As I said, love is at the very top of the pile. If you can access love, and hold love as a frequency or a vibration, even (and especially) become love, all of your shadows will be gone in one beat of the heart. This might sound weak, it might sound like some weedy platitude, but these are very powerful verbs; they are actual states of consciousness that I have experienced and experimented with. When love is accessed the lower emotions of depression and anger and hate cannot exist in the same body.

Humour

As a doorman faced with violence on a daily basis I developed a savage humour to combat fear. As well as being a high-frequency state, laughter also acts as a surrogate release for excess energy. As a man facing violence on a nightly basis I found that humour as an antidote worked, and it worked again and again, even if way back then I didn't exactly know why. I laughed more working in that life-threatening employ than I have ever laughed before or since.

Similarly, when I worked as a hod carrier on the building sites the conditions were savagely demanding, the work only attracted very tough men, and if they were not tough men they either developed hardiness or they did not survive. When your hands are bleeding from collisions and grazes and accidents with brick and block and scaffold (and sometimes with other workers) and the weather (inclement or otherwise) beats down on you like a slave master, humour (of the very black variety) is sometimes the only thing that keeps you going. I can remember driving to work in a van full of roughnecks at seven in the morning, after working until three the night before in a night club, and laughing so much that I cried.

Inspiration

When I was depressed as a twenty-year-old, working in the factory and scared of living, I read a book called *Watership Down* by Richard Adams. The book was wonderful and it filled me with so much hope and inspiration (the protagonist of the story was a rabbit called Hazel, who went on to lead his warren even though he was smaller than all the other rabbits. He was small in size, but massively courageous) that it acted as the catalyst that helped to pull me out of that dark place. Hope and inspiration and courage (borrowed from a fictitious rabbit) found my depression and dissolved it.

Loving honesty

When I was thirty and in a loveless marriage, living a hopeless life with no faith in myself and no happy future on the horizon (I could not even see a horizon), I met a girl called Sharon, who told me that I could be anything I wanted to be. She pointed out my great strengths of character and she also told me that my ugly and violent alter ego would always hold me back. Her loving honesty was the first heavy exposure that my shadow had to the beautiful poison, and ultimately the harbinger of its final doom.

Motivation

When my father died of cancer and my life was bouncing back and forth between rocks and very hard places and I was full of shadow, my friend Tony Terranova (www.fighting fit. gb.com) sent me a collection of motivational talks (40 hours' worth) by some of the most inspirational men and women in the world today. I diligently listened to an hour a day for a month and it lifted me out of that pit to a place high above my depression.

The motivation dissolved those shadows and filled me with strength.

Everything that is exposed to light itself becomes light, we have discovered this much already, but you can quicken this process with specific techniques. I'd like to look at these in the next chapter, Dissolving the Shadow.

Chapter 9

Dissolving the Shadow

In the previous chapters I have talked much about identifying, hunting and exposing the shadow. I have also touched upon specific techniques to dissolve the shadow and give it new life outside of your coil by using it as a creative energy. In this chapter I'd like to elaborate and share in more detail a few techniques that I've developed in this regard. As I said, and I don't mind repeating, the very moment you start addressing shadows, you are automatically bringing them into the light, and this is the very first stage in dissolving them. Even the act of writing down shadows exposes them to your conscious self, which automatically exposes them to light. Beware though; as I said earlier, while many of the surface shadows will come out with their hands up and not offer a fight, the deeper shadows will be very conniving. Not only will they do anything and everything within their power to evade exposure, they will also orchestrate things in your body and in your life to draw you away from your quest.

The conscious filter

The conscious mind can act like a filter, blocking any outgoing emotions that it thinks will represent you in a bad light to your family, friends and peers or to the world at large. This is especially so if the vacating shadow is not congruent with the personality that you wish to (or usually) present. Many people suppress shadows of past abuse because of shame. Others are embarrassed about expressing anger and rage in front of people who perhaps have never seen them angered or enraged. They fear that uncontrolled or naked emotion might disappoint people. Most folk keep their shadows under lock and key and only show the world an acceptable face because they fear being judged. It is a real individual who doesn't care about what others think of them, and it is a giant who can say, 'Actually, this is me, warts and all; you can take it or leave it.'

Psychosomatic illness is often the result of emotions left unexpressed; it is shadow at play. I have lost count of the number of times a shadow or trapped emotion, often suppressed or repressed anger or rage that I have carried for a while, has tried to come out, only to be forced back in again by my conscious guard. As I said shadows are energy that is surplus to a healthy body, so if you don't get it out, it will settle (and often move around) in your body, causing a block to the flow of natural energy. It is when this energy is denied a behavioural release that it starts to create problems, aches, pains and illness inside your body.

My shadows have often taken the internal shape of anger and rage, and this very strong emotion was created (but not shown to the outside world) by traumatic situations in my life. For instance, when my brother Ray died hideously from alcoholism and I had to watch his last moments, I was so fucking angry at him. That he had given up, that he had died young and left his kids, that he had hurt my mum and dad in his thoughtless living and his violent dying, and that he had ravaged me, his young, impressionable brother, a man that idolised him. But my anger confused me because it felt so inappropriate. My brother was dying and I was angry! It made no sense to me. I loved his bones, and I understood that his addiction was an illness, and that my brother was no longer rational and that he was not deliberately trying to hurt anyone. The confusion created massive conflict and guilt in me. I also felt very ashamed of my anger, so I didn't express it. I just shoved it back deep inside, where even I didn't have to look at it. I was also angry that people came to visit my brother pissed up. I kid you not. He was a young, dying alcoholic and they came to visit him in the hospital drunk, straight from the pub, and that made me so fucking furious that I nearly burst trying to hold it in. And in their inebriation they were so full of shit. These were people who loved him, they were people I loved, but I was still enraged. It's how they coped; these were drinking folk who dealt with their problems by going down the pub. They always had and they probably always would and I understood that, even if I didn't like or agree with it. My anger was not going to change their addictions or their bad behaviour. All the same it still made me furious. But the hospital where my brother was dying was not a good place for my uncontrolled rage. So that got shoved back as well.

Similarly, when my daughter took an overdose of painkillers and we thought we might lose her, I was so sad, but also very angry because her pain and her actions caused us all so much agony. And again I felt ashamed at being angry; it felt so selfish and narcissistic. I was also raging inside at her boyfriend, who was a thoughtless and ignorant man who came very close to getting battered by me. It took a lot of willpower not to go to his house and kick ten barrels of shit out of him.

My anger in both cases was a well of emotion that I never expressed at the time. It was inappropriate in both cases to lose my temper (and anyway, I was a man trying to be spiritual, and spiritual people do not lose their temper, do they?) so the energy got suppressed and many years later, long after I had forgotten my rage, I became depressed and ill and wasn't quite sure why. I spoke long and hard with a very close friend, a counsellor called Tony Somers (www.tonysomers.com). He said, 'Do you have any unexpressed anger?' I almost scoffed at the mere suggestion. 'No! Me? I'm spiritual, I don't get angry.' I genuinely didn't think I did. I couldn't locate one fluid ounce of anger in me, but when we spoke about my brother's death and how I felt about it a tsunami of almost uncontrollable rage welled up inside me. And when we spoke about the people who came to visit my brother in hospital, drunk, it started to spill, and suddenly I was in such a fury that every other word was a spitting, highly emotive expletive and my shadow spewed out. Up until that point I felt ashamed at my anger, and so I hid it, and in hiding it I created a strong shadow that became root-bound and later caused depression and psychosomatic illness. In my case the anger settled all around my groin area, from my lower stomach to my anus, and I suffered a lot of digestive problems and irritable bowel syndrome. When the energy settled in any one area I could actually feel it pulsating in my body, and the area would become red hot. Once I recognised the trapped emotion I started to express it through talking, through self-counselling and through writing and teaching. I 'outed' the feelings that I was ashamed of and the anger that I didn't want the world to see, and in telling the world I exposed my shadow. Over a short period of time I was able to exhaust (most of) the anger, until I was left with nothing but a deep and warm love for my brother, and compassion for those who couldn't cope with his death without alcoholic assistance. As for my daughter, I loved her so much that any unexpressed anger was quickly dissolved by the beautiful poison.

So the conscious filter can act like a jailer, keeping all the inmates in their cells, because it doesn't want the world at large to see any ugly representations of you. As the blocked emotions arise the conscious guard looks at them and makes an assessment: 'Do we want the world to see this? How will the world judge us?' And if the answer is in the negative, then it redirects the rage back inside, often so cunningly that you hardly even notice it happening. The energy will be left inside your body. It'll settle somewhere, usually in major areas like the back, the head, the groin, the stomach (different places for different people) and blocks the normal flow of energy. Hence we suffer with our backs, we get headaches, our stomachs bloat and so on. At one time or another I have felt my trapped emotions settle in just about every major area of my body and cause me discomfort, pain and sometimes out and out illness, until I addressed the shadow and got it out. I remember one time when it settled in my testicles and they throbbed like beacons. They felt like they were the size of coconuts. Deep down I knew it was psychosomatic, but I still whipped them out anyway and said to my wife, 'Is it just me, or do my bollocks look like coconuts?' She said they looked normal to her ('And please can you put them away now? We are in Sainsbury's.'), so I put them away and I took them to the doctors. Again I got them out, and I said the same thing: 'Testicles or coconuts?' My doctor checked me out and said that physically I was perfectly healthy, but... did I have any unexpressed anger? YES, I FUCKING DO, NOW THAT YOU MENTION IT!!! So again I found ways to express that anger and cleared my energy backlog.

As I said earlier, many of the emotions are so historical and so well repressed that you genuinely will not be aware of their existence, let alone their root cause. All you'll know is their manifestations, their children, and if you're brave and if you're diligent, you'll follow these right back to their cause (their mother, the shadow) and you'll address them. Also, once you understand the workings of the conscious filter, you can supervise it, and you can learn to override it, and when appropriate, let the trapped emotions speak.

Masterclass

On the six-month masterclass I teach for advanced self defence (the art of self defence against the self), I warn the students from the very first session that their shadows will emerge at regular intervals throughout the six-month course to try and stop them from attending the class. And invariably these shadows do arise and they do try to sabotage them; all sorts of wild and wonderful (sometimes dangerous) things happen to try and keep them away from exposure. Mysterious ailments and injuries will pop up; cars will break down or crash. One of the students told me that his car broke down on three separate occasions during the six-month course, and every time it happened on the very morning he was due to attend my class. Another man, struggling with some powerful shadows, took three goes (nearly two years) before he could actually complete the course. Others still found themselves interrupting every session (or their shadow interrupted every session) with intellectual smokescreens in a bid to challenge my teaching or avoid hearing the information that would jar their shadow free. So this is a course in courage, and patience and diligence; shadows are like seasoned enemies and will use fear, threat and artifice to stop you from exposing them.

This will be a challenging time, so keep your helmet straps tight.

Here are the methods I have used and developed to dissolve shadow.

Presence

Shadows cannot exist in the here and now. They feed on past recollections and future predictions. If you're present in your body consistently, shadows will dissolve of their own accord. When the shadow is hungry it will send out for a takeaway, and it will feed, and it will sustain itself and grow. The shadow will project out of the body and into the past where it gorges on either the pain or misery of historical injustices, or it will marinate in the happier past when times were better. An unschooled mind is like (as they say in Zen) a crazy monkey that will run riot if you don't learn to control it. And when it feeds, it gorges. Equally, the shadow will project forward and either feed on future fears and disasters and injustices (similar or worse than those experienced in the past) or it will marinate in fantastical liaisons with future success.

Society unconsciously helps to nurture your shadow by feeding you fear and pleasure in the form of pornographic TV, radio, newspapers and magazines, gossip and so on. We take all this in, thousands of times a day, and the stories and vignettes and racy images feed our urge to project, either forward to the promises that they hold or back to some kind of haven from the fears they threaten. The best way to stop these projections is to train your mind to stay present, train it not to project backwards and forwards in time. This can be done through the techniques described in earlier chapters, such as meditation, correct diet, eschewing the poor food choices (physical, cerebral and spiritual) that society offers, and finding your own source of sustenance. And also just by being in the arena and literally practising. When you have the urge to regress with your thoughts or project forward, when you have the urge to follow stories and images to the dark places of the unrestrained imagination, stop yourself by forcing the mind to stay present. You develop the muscles to do this by doing it. There is no magic. Just practice.

Focus

In Zen one of the things the students practise in order to stay present is the art of focus. People don't often realise that the mind is the most powerful tool we have, but it has to be trained. Because this is rarely taught in modern society we have forgotten (or we were never taught), and so the mind has become this crazy monkey that does exactly what it wants, when it wants and how it wants, and in the process it gets us into all sorts of trouble. Focus is one of the ways to calm the crazy monkey down and discipline it. The concept is simple enough: whatever you're doing, be present with it. If you are making a cup of tea, make a cup of tea; don't try and do ten other things at the same time, don't multi-task and don't daydream about the past and the future as you prepare your beverage. Be aware of every nuance in the tea-making ceremony; be in tune with every movement. Don't take your attention away from it, not even for a second. Resist the urge to let your mind drift; keep it busy on the art of making tea. When you do, making a cup of tea will become art, a pleasurable and uplifting experience, even a form of moving meditation. The same applies if you are painting a fence or if you are cooking a meal or having a conversation. If you are talking to someone, talk to them. Fully engage, stay present, listen to what they're saying, take your time with what you're saying, construct your sentences and make them thoughtful, artistic even. And don't let your eyes drift to someone else in the room, and definitely deny the urge to take phone calls or texts during the conversation. Again, this is all about practice. Next time you have a conversation try it and see how much more you get from the liaison and how much more the people you are talking to appreciate and respond to your undivided attention.

Drama therapy

This is why art and music and drama are now considered therapies, because when people engage in them, the very act of partaking becomes meditative. It keeps people entirely present, and in the present you are free from shadow, because it has no sustenance, it can't feed, and being constantly present is one of the main ways of dissolving shadow, without even identifying what your shadow might be. Also drama allows you to act out trapped emotions; it offers your shadow a legitimate way of temporarily being someone else and expressing things that the conscious filter would normally deny. It is a cunning way of sneaking the imprisoned emotions out of their fleshy jail in a dramatic disguise. And music is a snake charmer that puts the conscious guard to sleep while lulling out shadow on a cloud of soothing melody.

Writing this book is a focus that keeps me present; the act of bleeding my shadow through the keyboard and onto the screen is therapeutic, but also, for several hours every day, it keeps me entirely focused on the process. Writing demands no less; it keeps me fixed and in the now.

Out of body experience

Some people find ways of doing this naturally through hobbies and occupation, but more often than not the majority spend most of their incarnation out of the body, either in the past or in the future. This is not a profitable way to live; it is like having a luxury yacht at your disposal, but living instead in a dinghy in the sea. Even when I skip rope, I practise focus by keeping my mind on the rap of the leather as it hits the floor. When I run, I locate my breath and I follow it and this stops my mind from creating stories that feed shadow. Practise focus with everything you do, and even the most mundane tasks will become an exercise in Zen.

Stay in the luxury mansion that is your body. Don't waste your life living in a shitty, rented bedsit somewhere outside of you.

The power of now – the internal focus

Eckhart Tolle, in his groundbreaking book *The Power of Now*, talks a lot about focusing on the shadow itself when it emerges. He does this by locating the feelings of shadow (fear, guilt, shame, pain, anger, etc.) at the very moment they arise, before they can go into the story and have their feed.

He locks on to them, concentrates, and takes his mind into the very centre of the feelings, resisting every urge to project out and follow the story that feeds shadow. Once he is in the centre of the feeling he just sits there and observes. At the centre of all shadows we find the same thing: energy. If you go to the heart of that energy the moment it arises and focus on it, as though you have an inner eye that is actually looking at the feelings, it will dissolve. It might try and escape, you may feel the energy move to try and evade your inward focus, stay with it, follow it, corner it and lock on. The feelings rely on you panicking and following the story for their sustenance, so the moment you refuse to play this game they become powerless. This is a hugely effective technique. It takes courage because it means trying something new. We are so used to hiding from our feelings or panicking with our feelings, or following negative or fantastical stories until we feel ill, that this anti-intuitive technique of turning in instead of turning away might seem foreign at first, even scary, but with practice you'll see that it is very effective. The more you practise this, the easier and more effective it will become. Eventually you'll be able to dissolve any feelings that come up almost as soon as they arise. This will become your challenge: not to run from the feelings, not to follow negative or fantastical or pornographic stories, but to go to the centre of the feelings and dissolve them.

Killing the story

You have probably noticed that when your mind wanders and accesses the past or the future it creates a story. When these stories are frightening, generally negative and disproportionate, they don't serve us, they simply feed our shadow. They also take us out of the body, so that we are not living now, in the present. So we need to kill the story, and again we do this with diligence, focus and presence. As I said earlier, society is feeding us stories every minute of every day via the popular media, and nine times out of ten they are negative and debilitating. We tend to ingest these stories without questioning, because we don't know any better. If you follow the stories without resistance, they become an easy feed for shadow. Common stories all over the world's media are about the fear, violence and greed in society, economic crises, natural disasters, famine and war. They are on the news 24/7, and many people feed their shadow with the negative stories all day long, so much so that they become their whole reality. If you want to starve the shadow, kill the story. Kill it dead. Practise killing it. If you are in the company of a worry monger and he starts feeding you horror stories, stop him, and either change the story or change the company. If you are watching TV and the news is pulling you down with negativity (again), switch it off and engage yourself in a better story. There are plenty out there, you just have to look for them. Read a book. Watch a film. Ring a positive friend. Kill the story. You have the power to do this. And better still, feed your inspiration by finding or creating a better story, one that lifts you, and one that sustains you. Invest in books and CDs and DVDs that offer a better tale. I don't watch the news. I don't engage in negative conversations and I don't read disempowering tabloids. It is below my game.

I know that stories are often hard to stop in your head. But then it is hard to pick up weights and train every day, it is uncomfortable to go out for a run, and often painful to study for your exams. The good stuff is always hard; that's how you know it's good. You make it easier by practising whatever it is that you want to be good at. The mind is a muscle; make yours sinewy and svelte by giving it a hard daily workout.

The body conduit

The body is a conduit for light, or for God or for massive potential. Everything that we experience in the world, we experience through the physical body. Everything that we create in the world, we create through the physical body. With this in mind we can use the physical body as a way of behaviourally spending the shadow energy via physical creation. If you can captain yourself, if you can see your shadow as a reservoir of energy, if you can take the labels off that energy and draw from it, you can create prolifically. You can place the energy into your work, your relationships, your hobbies, even your passions. When I was young and more fearful than anyone I knew I was a very bipolar type character. I was either smashing up my house and punching holes in walls with my uncontrolled energy or I was bedbound and weeping with manic depression. I learned in time to control my massive fear and drive it into projects. Initially I placed my energy into physical training and that acted as an outlet for many of my surface shadows. As I released them I started to bump into the deeper, darker shadows and I needed a greater outlet than the physical training could offer. So I started to teach other people martial arts and self-reliance; this was a very worthy and profitable channel. And then when I went deeper still and the big guns emerged, I hit pay dirt, a geyser of shadow burst forth and I was forced once again to find an even greater vent than the ones I had thus far accessed. This outlet was (for me) writing. The physical training and teaching (which I was and I am still doing) offered a good but limited behavioural release for my shadow and it helped to keep me balanced. But it was the art of creative writing that acted as the ultimate conduit for energy that would not come out safely in any other way. This is when I really started to release some deep-seated shadows. The writing somehow bypassed my conscious filter and delved into the dark recesses of my unconscious and released shadows that I was not even aware I had. It was as though I had created a Colditz tunnel that enabled these trapped emotions to escape. And escape they did, in books, plays, articles, columns, newsletters, films, talks – it just kept coming and coming, and each book and each article and each film brought forth more black gold than the last, and with each word I wrote I became lighter and lighter, and each completed project that I put out into the world opened me up to further and greater release and earned me a bigger audience.

Releasing my own shadows helped other people to release theirs, and they in turn took the words and the ideas and passed them on.

What started as a bid to clear myself of shadow became an industry. I created an internal exodus; the shadows were queuing inside me waiting for their turn to leave, and find life in a book or a film. What began as a bid to hunt shadow became a beautiful source of creativity.

Transcendence

Some people find their catharsis through sport, others still in art and sculpture, many climb mountains to exorcise their shadows and some go into the healing arts. Most concur that shadows are not demons or monsters; they are frightened and trapped parts of our old self that want to leave, to transcend.

They just don't know how to do it. Our job is to find the how, and guide these great energies to a better place, in the process bringing ourselves to a better place.

Knowing this information will give you great hope; practising and experimenting with the techniques can change your life for ever. But this is not a one-shot deal. It is a path, and once you are on it you must stay on it; you must maintain what you've started or risk slipping back and allowing your shadows to re-establish themselves.

Chapter 10

Maintenance

Organisms that fail to grow, ultimately fail to live. Maintenance is about understanding the nature of growth and atrophy and working in accordance with it. In other words maintaining the work started. The universal law should be obvious to anyone who has spent any decent amount of time on earth: what we pay attention to grows and what we take attention away from will die. It is vital, therefore, that you continue with diligence what you have started because what you don't use you will lose. And, as is usually the case, if you don't maintain the work started the shadow will re-establish itself, bigger and stronger than before, and it will be better prepared for your next assault, should there ever be one. Making the decision and finding the purpose to hunt and dissolve your shadow once is hard enough, but to do it twice or more is asking for trouble. The most difficult aspect of this path is not the process itself; once you've found purpose and you begin, you build easy momentum and progress can escalate quite quickly. What is difficult, as I said at the beginning of the book, is finding the purpose. This can be a very difficult and lengthy process, so once you've found it please don't lose it again, because if you do the shadow will re-establish itself. Don't forget it knows the game now, so it will be better prepared to defend its occupancy. I've lost count of the amount of people I know who have cleared or partly cleared shadow, only to become complacent and fall off the path. I had one friend who took himself from a suicidal state to almost complete balance using these techniques, and then allowed impatient ambition, followed by a self-pitying melancholy to drag his bones right back to the start line again. And the last I heard he was still there, attacking anyone and everyone who was still on the path and accusing them of abandoning him. It is very easy when you're on this path to allow overconfidence and pride to enter the fray. In the latter case my friend did really well to begin with and his confidence was high, perhaps too high. After his initial triumphant encounters with old shadows he was now finding success in almost every area of his life, and he allowed himself to underestimate his shadow. He was celebrating before the fight was won, telling me how easy he was finding the journey now, and that he could achieve anything that I (or anyone else) had achieved. And of course that's true, he could, but at his stage of early development it would not be done quickly or without a longer gestation period. I'd won a BAFTA the previous year, and he announced out of the blue that he was going to win one himself by the following year. It had taken me fifteen years to make my first film, so while it's not impossible to reach this goal inside twelve months, it is improbable for a man still in the early stages of learning to write script. I encouraged him to write, but advised him not to be in such a hurry; he had a craft to learn and that could not be fast-tracked. His impatience reminded me of a story I once heard about a young student who was searching for camera-ready mastery; he wanted it and he wanted it now! Like many people, he wanted to have three before three had occurred. He said to his martial arts sensei, 'How long will it take me to become a master?' The sensei told him, 'Ten years.' The student looked perturbed. Ten years seems like a long time when you're in a rush. 'What if I train twice as hard and do twice as many hours?' he asked. 'Then it will take you twenty years,' the sensei replied. You can't rush nature. Plant a seed in the ground and give it ideal conditions and it will grow in its own season, but not before. The very act of rushing will delay the process.

My friend had mistaken my sage advice for jealous cautioning. He'd forgotten that I loved him, and that jealousy can't exit in the same orbit as love. Ignoring my counsel he got to work on his first script and he finished it very quickly. And when it failed to get past the first base, he became instantly disillusioned. I explained to him the nature of scriptwriting; most of the great work is done in the rewriting, and scripts can take a long time to mature. He threw the work away and got angry, telling me that he'd beat me to the next BAFTA (I wasn't even aware that we were in a race). Then he slowly started to allow bitterness to enter his mind, he felt sorry for himself, and he fed his acrimony and self-pity on an unhealthy diet of negative stories (about how everyone was jealous of him, about how the world was against him, and about how no one would give him a break in the film world), and suddenly the shadow reinstated itself and he was not just back to the start line, he was worse than ever before. Now he was in the position of having to find his purpose again, because his shadows, encamped and comfortable back inside him, had blocked his light, hidden his purpose and relegated him to a frequency in the lower echelons.

Another friend who struggled with many shadows was able through diligent practice to find his purpose, and he shone like a new torch. He recognised in a moment of clarity that he could do anything; nothing was impossible. And he was right, he could do anything and there are no impossibilities. But some things take time. If you want to build a big structure, you need a deep, wide base, and his base was still new and settling. He told me that he was going to change the world within a year; he was not going to become a millionaire, but a billionaire inside twelve months. Again, like the BAFTA, this is not impossible, but for a man who is still at the beginning of the game it is improbable. I tried to slow him down; I could see the signs, he had cleared some internal shadows, and he'd created a little light, but now he was being lured by the bling shadow that was seducing him and telling him, 'You can have it all, and you can have it now.' His walk changed – it went from humble and confident to bloated and arrogant – his manner transformed, he told his friends how he would surpass all his teachers inside a year, and his mind closed. Where before he was listening to those ahead of his game, now he was just scanning them for faults, and when he found any hint of brass in their feet he discounted them as teachers. Within six months this man had slipped back several degrees further than his original start point, and was once again scrabbling about in the dark, searching for the purpose to find his purpose.

I am sure that you've seen it a thousand times when folk lose weight and transform themselves into new people. Then they go on holiday and have a 'well-earned rest' from their diet, and they're back on the slippery slope to shadow.

The longer you work on evicting a shadow, the weaker that shadow becomes. Eventually it will leave you and it will be impotent. But, and this is a very important but, that shadow and a million more like it are always looking for a way back in and they will take any and every opportunity to do so. In the Christian religion it is taught that we should beware when we kick out our personal demons because they will try and come back again, with loads of their mates. It only takes a second of weakness for them to reinstate themselves. And once reinstated they will begin to quietly whisper in your ear and tempt you to feed them. Shadows have an insatiable appetite, so once the feeding starts and the frenzy begins it might never end.

Keep your helmet straps tight

The old Samurai had a saying: 'After the battle, tighten your helmet straps.' Your most vulnerable time is immediately after a conflict, when you think that the fight is won. A good sign that you are on your guard is when you consciously keep your helmet straps tight, you remain diligent and you give your opponent the respect he deserves. A bad sign is when you find yourself thinking, I've got this off now, I've mastered it, and so you loosen your helmet straps and relax. I shudder when I think back to my own mistakes and the times I've heard myself saying those exact words. 'Yeah, I've mastered diet, it's easy; I've got my addiction exactly where I want it,' and within a very short period of time I am lost again in some desert land without purpose and my shadows are clicking their portly finger and demanding a meal. Until, that is, I rediscovered my purpose and once again made myself an inhospitable host.

The weekend Mushasi

Do not underestimate shadow. I cannot repeat this often enough. And don't ever make the mistake of thinking that you can flirt with shadow, or compromise with shadow. Either your shadow is dead, or it is still a threat. There can be no middle ground. So be merciless. Get on the path, stay on the path, and dissolve any shadow that raises its head above the parapet. Keep in mind always that you are the master and not the slave, and make sure that any flirtation with shadow (because shadow will use any and every seduction as a loss leader to get you hooked) is killed dead. Flirtation is an insult to you; it is below your game. Flirtation is for the puppets whose strings are being pulled and controlled by the flavours of internal and external shadows. Either you are a full-time warrior or you are a weekend Mushasi, and working at the weekend is almost as bad as not working at all.

Epilogue

So there we are. This is what I have learned thus far, and this is my latest offering. I am learning and I am growing all the time, so I'll keep making literary contributions as I tighten my game. What I offer next may contradict what I have written in this and previous works, which I fully expect. Contradiction is good. As Mahatma Ghandi once said, 'My job is not to be consistent with the past, it is to be consistent with the truth.' And the truth changes with every new lesson I learn.

The good stuff in this book will resonate with you; it will speak to you on a level deeper than intellect because it will trigger truths that you already know; it will unearth knowledge that you have been carrying through many lifetimes in your genes and in your cells and in your soul. I am sure that at some points it will jar, even shock you. This is good. It means that a shadow has been unearthed, and a shadow is not real. Anything that can be threatened is not real. That's how you tell the difference between your true self and shadow.

You are an ancient being, many thousands of years old and you already know everything that you need to know, it just needs to be remembered. And study (that leads to self-study) will enable you to do just that. It is my belief that the darker shadows that we harbour do not want us to access this elixir, because the truth will set you free, which spells the end of their existence. And this is perhaps why we are so often disinclined to sit down and study. We are always being distracted by the inclinations of superficially alluring things, which feed the shadow and block the light of realisation.

I always feel that when I study I do so to learn what I already know. In Plato's *Protagoras and Meno* (Penguin Classics) the author demonstrates through two dialogues that learning is not just the simple process of being instructed by a master or by a teacher, rather it is a process of being helped to 'bring up from within' knowledge and information which the soul has learned before birth and forgotten.

It is my hope that this text will help you to remember what you already know.

Good hunting.

The Beginner's Guide to

DARKNESS

This Book will Help you to Find the Light

GEOFF THOMPSON